DAY BY DAY
with followers of francis & clare

Pat McCloskey, O.F.M.

Foreword by Murray Bodo, O.F.M.

ST. ANTHONY MESSENGER PRESS

Cincinnati, Ohio

Nihil Obstat: Rev. Donald Miller, O.F.M.

Imprimi Potest: Rev. John Bok, O.F.M.

Some of the individuals in this volume are neither canonized nor beatified. The author defers to the Church's formal judgment on the holiness of those men and women.

The first edition of this work was published as *Franciscan Saint of the Day,* copyright ©1981 by St. Anthony Messenger Press.

Quotations from the writings of Saint Francis are taken from *Francis and Clare: The Complete Works,* by Regis Armstrong, O.F.M. Cap., and Ignatius Brady, O.F.M., copyright ©1982 and from *Bonaventure: The Soul's Journey Into God, The Tree of Life, The Life of St. Francis,* copyright ©1978, are used by permission of Paulist Press. All rights reserved.

Quotations from *1 Celano, 2 Celano,* the *Legenda Major* and the *Mirror of Perfection* are taken from *St. Francis of Assisi: Writings and Early Biographies, English Omnibus of the Sources for the Life of St. Francis,* edited by Marion Habig, O.F.M., copyright ©1977, and *The Franciscan Book of Saints,* by Marion Habig, O.F.M., copyright ©1979, by Franciscan Herald Press are used by permission. All rights reserved.

Cover painting by Darina Gladišová, *Spiritual Friendship of St. Francis and St. Clara,* copyright ©1998

Cover design by Sanger & Eby Design
Book design by Constance Wolfer

ISBN 0-86716-336-4

Published by St. Anthony Messenger Press
Printed in the U.S.A.

Contents

* Commemorated on the Franciscan calendar
+ Commemorated on the Roman calendar

———

Acknowledgments

Francis of Assisi told his followers that their willingness to beg if necessary would make them "rich in virtue" (Rule of 1223, *Omnibus* text). That willingness to beg is one form of the self-emptying demanded of those who seek to live out the gospel. Over 770 years after his death the truth of that prediction is obvious. The Franciscan family is constantly providing new examples of holiness, of living out the Good News of Jesus in a great variety of ways.

This book was first published in June 1981 under the title *Franciscan Saint of the Day*. I want to explain some changes and add the thank-yous incurred in revising the text and including the nine Franciscans canonized and the twenty-one Franciscans beatified since 1980. Two Franciscans in the previous volume have been declared venerable since 1980.

A considerable number of people mentioned in this book have been beatified and/or canonized by Pope John Paul II. The quotes from his homilies on those occasions have been taken from the weekly English-language edition of *L'Osservatore Romano*. Year, issue number and page number are given in the citation. For example, 1996 LOR 23:1 means Number 23, page one of the 1996 volume of *L'Osservatore Romano*.

Besides the new saints and blesseds, I have added two deceased friars whom I knew and whom I considered to be holy. A few changes have been made in the Glossary on pages 5 and 6.

I am grateful to Mary Schroeder of St. Francis Bookshop (Cincinnati, Ohio) and Joe Rayes, O.F.M., for encouraging St. Anthony Messenger Press to request a revision of the first edition. Murray Bodo, O.F.M., graciously agreed to write the Foreword for this new edition. Patti Normile, Mary Lynne Rapien and Barbara Sonnenberg improved my entry on their friend Leonard Foley, O.F.M. Margaret Carney, O.S.F., did the same for the one on Ignatius Brady, O.F.M.

Luca De Rosa, O.F.M., postulator general at the Friars Minor international headquarters in Rome, provided valuable data regarding Franciscans beatified and/or canonized since 1980. The staff of our provincial archives (Friars Dan Anderson, Don Rewers and Marcan Hetteberg) offered valuable assistance as did the periodical and reference librarians at Xavier University in Cincinnati.

I also wish to acknowledge my debts to those who contributed to the first editon of this book.

I am especially grateful to Father Ignatius Brady, O.F.M., who taught me at the Franciscan Institute (St. Bonaventure University) and who, despite a busy schedule, agreed to write a Foreword to the 1981 volume.

Helping me to draw up a list of people to be included in the book were Fathers Nicholas Lohkamp, O.F.M., Larry Landini, O.F.M., Regis Armstrong, O.F.M. Cap., Salvator Fink, O.F.M., and Sister Mary McCarrick, O.S.F.

The following Franciscan sisters (O.S.F.) provided valuable information about the founders of their congregations: Frances Elizabeth, Veronica Inez Rodrigues, Lois Ann, Margaret Eugene, Elaine Kerscher, Mary Laurence Hanley, Sabina Collins, Lauretta Mather, Francis Assisi Kennedy and Donna Marie Woodson. Sister Anna, O.S.C., and Sister Mary Emelita, C.S.S.F., provided similar information for their congregations. I am also grateful for information provided by Fathers Marion Habig, O.F.M., Roy Effler, O.F.M., and Louis Secondo, T.O.R., and Brother Leo Wollenweber, O.F.M. Cap.

My thanks also go to Father Jeremy Harrington, O.F.M., who proposed the book and to Carol Luebering and Father Greg Friedman, O.F.M., who edited it.

Finally, I am indebted to the Franciscans of the Province of St. John the Baptist (Cincinnati) and to all the other members of the Franciscan family who have lived the gospel of Jesus with infectious joy and generosity.

Pat McCloskey, O.F.M.

Foreword to the Revised Edition

When Saint Francis was dying, he covered Christ's wound in his side — as though to seal the uniqueness of his own response to God — and said to his brothers, "I have done what was mine to do; may Christ teach you what you are to do" (2 *Celano*, #214).

And so the Lord did, and how marvelous has been that showing. Holy men and women as diverse in background and personality as Saint Thomas More and Blessed Angela of Foligno, Saint Agnes of Prague and Saint Paschal Baylon, have found within the way of Saint Francis their own unique way to walk in the footprints of Jesus. Saint Francis himself used to say that his followers were to "walk in the footprints of Christ" rather than "imitate Christ," thereby emphasizing each person's unique response instead of a blind and mindless imitation.

And this is how the followers of Saint Francis are to walk: "The rule and life of the Friars Minor is this: to observe the holy Gospel of our Lord Jesus Christ by living in obedience, without anything of their own, and in chastity." How these words are lived out is as various as those who live them, but all the followers of Francis are the same in that the Poor Savior is the shared love, the sole model of what it means to be holy. The Poor Savior Jesus Christ, "who, though he was in the form of God, did not regard equality with God as something to be exploited, but emptied himself, taking the form of a slave, being born in human likeness. And being found in human form, he humbled himself and became obedient to the point of death — even death on a cross" (Philippians 2:6-8).

Franciscan observance of the holy gospel means that whatever has been excluded, broken, damaged, is to be included, healed, repaired, just as Saint Francis repaired churches, embraced lepers, included the poor and marginal in his love. And everything is to be observed as minors, *lesser* ones. At the time of Saint Francis society was divided (as it still is) into the *majores* and the *minores*, the "greaters" and the "lessers," and Saint Francis, in response to the Poor Christ, aligned himself and his followers with the "lessers."

The Franciscan way, as it has been lived from the beginning, can be described thus: Franciscans are poor, wandering, preaching brothers and sisters of penance. The lives whose stories constitute this book show concretely how the brothers and sisters of Francis are people of penance, how they have continued to live *poor* lives among the poor and marginal, how they have witnessed to the gospel *on the road*, so to speak, by the sermons their lives preach, and how *penance*, or *metanoia* (turning their own lives around and helping others turn their lives from sin to love of God and neighbor) has been the configuration of the Franciscan charism throughout the eight hundred years since the birth of Saint Francis and of Saint Clare, the first Franciscan woman.

From the onset the Franciscan way has included men *and* women. Saint Clare, a woman from the *majores*, in a gesture like that of Saint Francis himself, democratized her monastery of San Damiano by insisting on the equality and voice of all her sisters no matter what social class they belonged to previous to entering the monastery. Nor did Clare lord it over her sisters like the high-born woman she was; rather she served her sisters' needs, even washing their feet like the Poor Christ, who washed the feet of his disciples. Living incarnations of the Lady Poverty, Saint Clare and her sisters were the first to make the inclusion of women central to the Franciscan presence in the world.

Today Franciscan women and men work closely together in the work of evangelization and more importantly in reminding each other, and those whose lives they touch, of the importance of gender inclusion as a model of Church as we approach the twenty-first century. For conversion is not simply a turning from sin to God. It involves a radical change of attitudes as well. Sin separates, and grace brings together not just the soul separated from God, but whatever one has excluded from God's redeeming love, whether that be people we have excluded from our life because of their gender or social standing, or because their viewpoints differ from our own. The Franciscan way stretches the envelope of inclusion by "preaching the Gospel to every creature," as Saint Francis put it. *Every* creature, for the very name, "creature," says it was created by God. And everything created by God has been redeemed and sanctified by God. Franciscan preaching simply reminds all of creation of the truth that everyone and everything is included in God's creating, redeeming and sanctifying love. Conversion, then, or penance, means letting God turn one's self-centered life around in order to start living the implications of what it means to be created, redeemed and sanctified by a loving God.

Holy women and men grace these pages. Some are canonized saints, some blesseds, some venerables and a few are holy people not yet officially recognized as such by the Church; but all are examples of true conversion. Their very lives become the gospel they preach. Like Saint Francis and Saint Clare the gestures their lives make speak more clearly and movingly than do their words. And in that they are truly *Franciscan* models of holiness. They do, instead of just talking about doing, or recounting what others before them did. They heed the words of their Holy Father Saint Francis: "The sheep of the Lord followed Him in tribulation and persecution, in insult and hunger, in infirmity and temptation, and in everything else, and they have received everlasting life from the Lord because of these things. Therefore, it is a great shame for us, servants of God, that while the saints [actually] did such things, we wish to receive glory and honor by [merely] recounting their deeds" (*Admonition VI*).

May this book be more than an accounting of what saintly people have done; may it move us to follow, like them, in the footsteps of Our Lord Jesus Christ. And may our following be simple and humble like that of these holy Franciscans and Saint Francis himself, who said: "God has called me by the way of simplicity and humility, and has in truth revealed this way for me and for all who are willing to trust and follow me. So I do not want you to quote any other Rule to me, whether that of Saint Benedict, Saint Augustine, or Saint Bernard, or to recommend any other way or form of life except this way which God in His mercy has revealed and given to me. The Lord told me that He wished me to be a new kind of simpleton in this world, and He does not wish us to live by any other wisdom but this" (*Mirror of Perfection*, #68).

Murray Bodo, O.F.M.

Foreword to the First Edition

"Why after you? Why after you?" asks Brother Masseo of Francis. "...You are not a very handsome man, nor possessed of great learning or wisdom. So why is all the world running after you?" (*Little Flowers of St. Francis*, Ch. 10).

Brother Masseo, much beloved by Francis, was not above teasing his Father — as a test, one might say, of his humility. So, half-jokingly, Masseo posed this question to Francis one day as he returned from prayer.

Masseo knew the answer full well! All the world flocked after Brother Francis because he was like another Christ come among us to make the Good News come alive again in human hearts. Francis, however, gave Masseo quite a different answer: that God could not find anyone more vile or of less worth than he to put to shame the wise and to bring to nought those who were the great and strong among the children of Adam.

Both were right, for indeed both gave the same answer. Francis called on the words of the Apostle: "But God chose what is foolish in the world to shame the wise; God chose what is weak in the world to shame the strong; God chose what is low and despised in the world, things that are not, to reduce to nothing things that are...." (1 Corinthians 1:27-28). Masseo saw in Francis another John the Baptist — the name Francis received in Baptism — sent to call the People of God to repentance and to newness of life in Christ.

What happened by the grace of God during the lifetime of Saint Francis (1181/1182-1226), the Lord in his mercy and graciousness has let happen these last seven centuries and more in the hearts of men and women of all cultures, ages and climes. Why after you, Brother Francis, such a great crowd of men and women — priests, religious, laity, great and small, known or forgotten by the world? Why, save that through Francis Christ Jesus came alive to men and women of all ages since: Christ who humbled himself, taking the form of a servant, our form! Christ of the crib, Christ of the hidden life; Christ the shepherd, the teacher, the preacher; Christ in the grace-filled lives of men and women and to the point that almost daily, apart from the feasts of the Lord, of our Lady and of the apostles, our calendar could present the whole year round the sons and daughters of the little man of Assisi who in most varied ways came to Christ with him.

There was and still is a quality of uncertainty about the life of Francis' first followers, the Lesser Brothers: rooted in God, yet with no fixed abode on earth; rich in virtues, perhaps, but utterly poor in the things of this world; wise in the ways of God, yet foolhardy in the eyes of the people they met and sought to bring to the light of the gospel.

By their prayer and example, the friars showed all people how to live the Christian life in the midst of good times and bad, for Francis insisted that they live the gospel in a spirit of joy, inspired by such a deep love that they would hold back nothing for themselves, but give their very life and being and action completely to the Lord, the true and highest good, who alone is "good, merciful and gentle, holy, just and true" (*Rule of 1221*, Ch. 23).

Each year at the feast of Pentecost, the friars used to return to Assisi for a general meeting. On these occasions Francis gave his Admonitions which, although they were originally intended for the friars, are in great part a kind of practical manual of Christian life. Some few, indeed, explicitly touch on the life of a friar or religious; the rest nonetheless have very much to say to any serious follower of Francis in matters touching a truly Christlike life. They reveal how conscious Brother Francis was of the duties of every state of Christian life, and of Christ as the model for each and every one who glories in his name.

Small wonder then that this volume presents a great variety of saints and blessed and holy people of every age and clime who, from the thirteenth century to our own day, have found in Francis, in Clare and in the saints of the Third Order (now known as the Secular Franciscan Order) the inspiration and the encouragement to live totally for the Lord in the most varied circumstances of life, in good days and ill. Each in turn has obeyed the command the Lord gave the Little Man of Assisi: "Repair my house" — restore and strengthen my Church by your life, by your example, by taking up your cross daily to follow me, and by your death if need be in martyrdom, in witness to me by your very blood shed for all people in union with my cross.

"Therefore, it is a great shame for us servants of God that while the saints [actually] did such things, we wish to receive glory and honor by [merely] recounting their deeds" (Saint Francis, Admonition VI). Rather, may the Spirit of the Lord work in us, that in some small way we may follow them in the brotherhood and the littleness which is the way of Saint Francis.

Ignatius Brady, O.F.M.

Introduction

One day when the first followers of Francis were few and somewhat downhearted, he told them that the Lord would turn their company into "a very great multitude" (*1 Celano*, #27). And so God has.

This book will introduce people interested in Francis of Assisi to a few of the saintly men and women who make up the "multitude" of the Franciscan family that spans the eight hundred plus years from Francis' birth to our own day.

Each entry consists of a brief biographical sketch, a quote either from the person or about the person, and a comment on some aspect of the person's life particularly relevant to a follower of Francis today. Saints and blesseds are listed on the days indicated by the Franciscan calendar. Others are assigned to the day of their death or a nearby date if that day is already taken. The Roman numerals after their names indicate to which part of the Franciscan family they belong: First, Second or Third Order. (See the Glossary for these and other Franciscan terms.)

The Church permits individual religious communities to have their own calendars as long as they do not conflict with the Roman calendar for the worldwide Church. In 1973 the Friars Minor, Friars Minor Conventual, Friars Minor Capuchin, Third Order Regular of St. Francis, the Secular Franciscan Order and the Poor Clares submitted a common Franciscan calendar for approval by the Holy See. All of the saints on that calendar (see pages 159-161) are in this book. I have also included a representative sample of Franciscan blesseds. Other men and women not on the Franciscan calendar have been added to reflect Franciscans of the nineteenth and twentieth centuries, especially those who have been influential in the United States.

There is no composite Franciscan saint; indeed, there are no uniquely "Franciscan" virtues. There are simply men and women who have been inspired by the courage of Francis to risk everything in following Jesus. The holy followers of Francis do share, I believe, the following similarities worth our prayerful reflection:

- They are humble. One of Francis' favorite sayings was, "What a man is before God, that he is and nothing more" (*Admonition XIX*). For Francis, humility was the whole truth about God, himself and other creatures.

  Some of Francis' holy followers have been well known by their contemporaries. Others have lived and died in obscurity. In several of his Admonitions, Francis warns the friars not to be hungry for fame or publicity, but rather to be generous followers of Jesus.

- They are devoted to Christ's passion and cross. The holy followers of Francis have all realized that Jesus' path leads to the cross and through it to glory. There are no shortcuts.

- They practice penance. The sons and daughters of Francis have seen mortification as essential to gospel living. Penance helped them separate the baggage of their lives from the demands of the gospel.

  The penances of some holy Franciscans may strike us as bizarre; we may be inclined to dismiss these actions as those of people with very poor self-images. But Francis knew how easy it is for our "needs" to multiply.

- They have an innovative spirit. "Let us begin, brothers, to serve the Lord God, for up to now we have made little or no progress" was advice characteristic of the Poverello. According to Thomas of Celano, Francis was "always new, always beginning again." Why?

  The gospel of Jesus does not change from day to day. But a person's ability to live out the gospel can and should grow. Francis was a very creative man who tried various approaches with people until he found one which helped them see things from God's perspective.

- They are loyal to the Church. In the twelfth and thirteenth centuries there were many people who, like Francis, saw the Church as needing more poor, humble preachers of the gospel. Francis, however, clearly saw the inseparable bond between Scripture and the Church. While some reformers were patronizing to this clumsy, sinful contemporary Church and loved only the sleek and spotless Church yet to come, Francis worked with what he had.

- They have a missionary spirit. Part of Francis' innovative spirit was his concern for bringing the Good News to the Muslims, to a world where Christ had never been preached. His followers took the gospel to distant continents and many shed their blood to nourish its growth.

- They are devoted to the Eucharist. Francis saw the Eucharist as the unique place where God and his people meet. There the Lord of the Universe offers his own life to his creatures. Some saintly followers of Francis have daily prayed for hours before the Eucharist. All Franciscans know this awesome gift is the real power behind their work — whether preaching, caring for the sick or raising a family.

- They have great reverence for life. Francis and the men and women he inspired have helped us to see the unity of all creation. Whereas later romantics have often depicted Francis as more at home with birds and deer than with people, the truth is that Francis prized those animals for the same reason he valued all people — men and women, rich and poor, the healthy and the sick, Christian and non-Christian. God is to be praised in all creation.

- They are filled with joy. At first, it may seem odd that Francis was both penitential and yet full of joy. His penances were a part of the truth in his life; he showed respect for things by using them sparingly. No stranger to penance, Francis was one of the most joyful people who ever lived. His saintly followers have tried to follow that same path.

- They are busy but centered. Francis worked hard, preaching, consoling, praying, performing the corporal and spiritual works of mercy. His saintly followers have also been hard workers. But their work has not led to distraction or anger because it has always been related to God's overall plan for the world.

- They are "together" people. When we speak of holy men and women, we tend to highlight several virtues considered typical of each. In fact, the virtues grow together. To show that, Francis wrote *The Salutation of the Virtues*:

Hail, Queen Wisdom, may the Lord protect you
    with your sister, holy pure Simplicity.
Lady, holy Poverty, may the Lord protect you
    with your sister, holy Humility.
Lady, holy Charity, may the Lord protect you
    with your sister, holy Obedience.
O most holy virtues, may the Lord protect all of you,
    from whom you come and proceed.
There is surely no one in the entire world
    who can possess any one of you
    unless he dies first.
Whoever possesses one [of you]
    and does not offend the others,
    possesses all.
And whoever offends one [of you]
    does not possess any

and offends all.
And each one destroys vices and sins.
Holy Wisdom destroys
    Satan and all his subtlety.
Pure holy Simplicity destroys
    all the wisdom of this world
    and the wisdom of the body.
Holy Poverty destroys
    the desire of riches
    and avarice
    and the cares of this world.
Holy Humility destroys pride
    and all the people who are in the world
    and all things that belong to the world.
Holy Charity destroys
    every temptation of the devil and of the flesh
    and every carnal fear.
Holy Obedience destroys
    every wish of the body and of the flesh
    and binds its mortified body
        to obedience of the Spirit
        and to obedience of one's brother
and [the person who possesses her] is subject and submissive
    to all persons in the world
    and not to man only
    but even to all beasts and wild animals
    so that they may do whatever they want with him
    inasmuch as it has been given to them from above
    by the Lord.

May the holy men and women included in these pages inspire you to live the gospel of Jesus Christ with greater courage and joy!

Glossary

Admonitions: Instructions Saint Francis gave year by year to the friars who gathered for meetings in Assisi.

Blessed: A person whose life has been formally examined and confirmed in holiness as a stage in the canonization process. The title is given by the pope and allows veneration limited to a particular group or locality.

Capuchins: A group of Franciscan men who began in 1528 with permission to live a strict interpretation of the Rule of Saint Francis; identified by the initials O.F.M. Cap. (See also "First Order.")

Chapter: A meeting of Franciscans held at some definite interval on a local, provincial or general (worldwide) level.

Conventuals: A group of Franciscan men (sometimes called the "Black Franciscans" because of the color of their habits) differing from the Observant Franciscans in the interpretation of the vow of poverty and sometimes in the type of apostolate. They became a distinct group in 1517; initials are O.F.M. Conv. (See also "First Order.")

Custody: A geographical subdivision of a province, headed by a custos.

First Order: Franciscan men belonging to the Order of Friars Minor, the Order of Friars Minor Conventual or the Order of Friars Minor Capuchin.

Friar: A general term for a member of a mendicant or begging order (Franciscans, Dominicans, Augustinians and Carmelites); in this volume the term designates Franciscans.

Friary: The place where friars live.

Guardian: Originally another term for minister; now refers to superiors in designated houses.

Minister: The term Saint Francis used rather than superior; designates leaders on the local, provincial or general (worldwide) level.

Observants: A group of Franciscan men who separated from the Conventuals in 1517; sometimes called the "Brown Franciscans" because of the color of their habits. In 1897, Pope Leo XIII united several Observant subgroups to form the Order of Friars Minor; initials are O.F.M. (See also "First Order.")

Prefect Apostolic: The head of a missionary territory, appointed by the Holy See. Usually not a bishop.

Provincial: Short form of provincial minister, the major superior of a province, a territorial unit of the First Order.

Rule: A document describing the vision and purpose of a particular religious community; approved by the bishop for his diocese or by the pope for the entire Church.

Rule of 1209: Saint Francis' short document — now lost — approved verbally by Pope Innocent III; it consisted mostly of Gospel texts.

Rule of 1221: Saint Francis' first attempt at writing a comprehensive Rule; long, prayerful, somewhat rambling; never submitted to the pope. Also known as the Earlier Rule.

Rule of 1223: The short and concise Rule prepared by Saint Francis and the friars; approved by Pope Honorius III on November 29, 1223. Also known as the Later Rule.

Second Order: Cloistered Franciscan women following the Rule of Saint Clare.

Secular Franciscan Order: Formerly called the Third Order, a group of men and women, married or single, who follow a special Rule written by Saint Francis in 1221. Diocesan priests are also among its members.

Tertiary: A member of the Third Order Secular (Secular Franciscan Order) or Third Order Regular of Saint Francis; the term comes from *tertius,* the Latin word for "third."

Third Order Regular: A group of men who follow the Third Order Rule of Saint Francis and who live in religious communities; received papal approval in 1447 but ultimately trace their roots to Saint Francis; initials are T.O.R. Congregations of Franciscan sisters or brothers are related to the Third Order Regular by virtue of their founders' devotion to the Franciscan ideal. These congregations have more structured constitutions based on Franciscan values. In this book, women or men who belong to these congregations are identified by the "III" appearing after their name.

Third Order Secular: See "Secular Franciscan Order."

Venerable: A person who has completed the first step in the canonization process.

DAY BY DAY

with followers of francis & clare

Blessed Angela of Foligno (III)
1248-1309

Some saints show marks of holiness very early. Not Angela! Born of a leading family in Foligno, she became immersed in the quest for wealth and social position. As a wife and mother, she continued this life of distraction.

Around the age of forty she recognized the emptiness of her life and sought God's help in the Sacrament of Penance. Her Franciscan confessor helped Angela to seek God's pardon for her previous life and to dedicate herself to prayer and the works of charity.

Shortly after her conversion, her husband and children died. Selling most of her possessions, she entered the Secular Franciscan Order. She was alternately absorbed by meditating on the crucified Christ and by serving the poor of Foligno as a nurse and beggar for their needs. Other women joined her in a religious community.

At her confessor's advice, Angela wrote her *Book of Visions and Instructions*. In it she recalls some of the temptations she suffered after her conversion; she also expresses her thanks to God for the Incarnation of Jesus. This book and her life earned for Angela the title "Teacher of Theologians." She was beatified in 1693.

Quote: Pope John Paul II writes: "Christ the Redeemer of the World is the one who penetrated in a unique, unrepeatable way into the mystery of the human person and entered our 'hearts.' Rightly therefore does the Second Vatican Council teach: 'The truth is that only in the mystery of the Incarnate Word does the mystery of the human person take on light.... Christ the New Adam, in the very revelation of the mystery of the Father and his love, fully reveals human beings to themselves and brings to light their most high calling'" (*Redemptor Hominis*, 8).

Comment: People who live in the United States today can understand Blessed Angela's temptation to increase her sense of self-worth by accumulating money, fame or power. Striving to possess more and more, she became more and more self-centered. When she realized she was priceless because she was created and loved by God, she became very penitential and very charitable to the poor. What had seemed foolish early in her life now became very important. The path of self-emptying she followed is the path all holy men and women must follow.

Saint Berard and Companions (I)
d. 1220

Preaching the gospel is often dangerous work. Leaving one's homeland and adjusting to new cultures, governments and languages is difficult enough; but martyrdom sometimes caps all the other sacrifices.

In 1219 with the blessing of Saint Francis, Berard left Italy with Peter, Adjute, Accurs, Odo and Vitalis to preach in Morocco. En route in Spain Vitalis became sick and commanded the other friars to continue their mission without him.

They tried preaching in Seville, then in Muslim hands, but made no converts. They went on to Morocco where they preached in the marketplace. The friars were immediately apprehended and ordered to leave the country; they refused. When they began preaching again, an exasperated sultan ordered them executed. After enduring severe beatings and declining various bribes to renounce their faith in Jesus Christ, the friars were beheaded by the sultan himself on January 16, 1220.

These were the first Franciscan martyrs. When Francis heard of their deaths, he exclaimed, "Now I can truly say that I have five Friars Minor!" Their relics were brought to Portugal where they prompted a young Augustinian canon to join the Franciscans and set off for Morocco the next year. That young man was Anthony of Padua (June 13). These five martyrs were canonized in 1481.

Quote: Before Saint Francis, the Rules of religious orders made no mention of preaching to the Muslims. In the Rule of 1223, Francis wrote: "Those brothers who, by divine inspiration desire to go among the Saracens and other nonbelievers should ask permission from their ministers provincial. But the ministers should not grant permission except to those whom they consider fit to be sent" (Chapter 12).

Comment: The deaths of Berard and his companions sparked a missionary vocation in Anthony of Padua and others. There have been many, many Franciscans who have responded to Francis' challenge. Proclaiming the gospel can be fatal, but that has not stopped the Franciscan men and women who even today risk their lives in many countries throughout the world.

Saint Charles of Sezze (I)
1613-1670

C harles thought that God was calling him to be a missionary in India, but he never got there. God had something better for this seventeenth-century successor to Brother Juniper (January 28).

Born in Sezze, southeast of Rome, Charles was inspired by the lives of Salvator Horta (March 18) and Paschal Baylon (May 17) to become a Franciscan; he did that in 1635. Charles tells us in his autobiography, "Our Lord put in my heart a determination to become a lay brother with a great desire to be poor and to beg alms for his love."

Charles served as cook, porter, sacristan, gardener and beggar at various friaries in Italy. In some ways, he was "an accident waiting to happen." He once started a huge fire in the kitchen when the oil in which he was frying onions burst into flames.

One story shows how thoroughly Charles adopted the spirit of Saint Francis. The superior ordered Charles — then porter — to give food only to traveling friars who came to the door. Charles obeyed this direction; simultaneously the alms to the friars decreased. Charles convinced the superior the two facts were related. When the friars resumed giving goods to all who asked at the door, alms to the friars increased also.

At the direction of his confessor Charles wrote his autobiography, *The Grandeurs of the Mercies of God*. He also wrote several other spiritual books. He made good use of his various spiritual directors throughout the years; they helped him discern which of Charles' ideas or ambitions were from God. Charles himself was sought out for spiritual advice. The dying Pope Clement IX called Charles to his bedside for a blessing.

Charles had a firm sense of God's providence. Father Severino Gori has said, "By word and example he recalled in all the need of pursuing only that which is eternal" (Leonard Perotti, *St. Charles of Sezze: An Autobiography*, page 215).

He died at San Francesco a Ripa in Rome and was buried there. Pope John XXIII canonized him in 1959.

Quote: Father Gori says that the autobiography of Charles "stands as a very strong refutation of the opinion, quite common among religious people, that saints are born saints, that they are privileged right from their first appearance on this earth. This is not so. Saints become saints in the usual way, due to the generous fidelity of their correspondence to divine grace. They had to fight just as we do, and more so, against their passions, the world and the devil" (*St. Charles of Sezze: An Autobiography*, page viii).

Comment: The drama in the lives of the saints is mostly interior. Charles' life was spectacular only in his cooperation with God's grace. He was captivated by God's majesty and great mercy to all of us.

Saint Eustochia Calafato (II)
1430-c.1485

Eustochia shows us what freedom for God might mean. Born into a noble family in Messina (Sicily), Smaragda resisted her father's attempts to arrange a marriage for her. At the age of sixteen, she entered a nearby Poor Clare monastery, receiving the name Eustochia. During her eleven years in that monastery, she cared for the sick sisters, once even nursing those afflicted by the plague.

Seeking to live the Rule of Saint Clare more strictly, she founded a monastery for that purpose in 1460. Four years later it relocated to Montevergine, where Eustochia served several terms as abbess.

Eustochia was devoted to Mary and to the passion of Jesus. Her intercession is invoked against earthquakes. Known also as Eustochia of Messina, she was canonized in 1988.

Quote: Explaining liberation as a biblical theme, Archbishop Desmond Tutu once wrote: "People are set free *from* bondage to the world, the Devil and sin, in order to be free *for* God, and to be fully human because Christ came that they might have life in its abundant fullness" (Desmond Tutu, *Hope and Suffering*, page 58).

Comment: Cloistered life was where Eustochia became free for God — free from societal and family pressures as well as free from her own temptation to boss God around. Inside or outside a monastery, each of us must face the false gods which promise us freedom but deliver only bondage.

Juan de Padilla (I)
1492-1542

Juan didn't know where preaching the gospel of Jesus would lead him, but he trusted God to give him strength to match the missionary vocation. Juan's vocation led to his martyrdom in Kansas, part of the New World discovered the year he was born.

Juan came from southern Spain where he became a Franciscan. In 1526 he left for Mexico where he worked as a missionary in the states of Hidalgo and Jalisco. In 1540 he accompanied Coronado's expedition to New Mexico. The next year Juan went with the expedition to Kansas; there he met the Quivira Indians. Juan remained to work among them after the explorers returned to Mexico.

Juan was killed by several Quivira Indians as he made his way to the Kaws, traditional enemies of the Quiviras. He was the first of at least seventy-nine Franciscans martyred in the United States.

Quote: An ad for missionaries in a nineteenth-century Paris newspaper also applied to Juan's work: "We offer you no salary, no recompense, no leadership, no pension, but much hard work, a poor dwelling, small consolation, many disappointments, frequent sickness, a violent or lonely death and an unknown grave."

Comment: Thinking about people who are martyrs for the faith sometimes makes us uncomfortable. How could people do that? Are they mentally stable? Juan de Padilla was motivated more by a desire to spread the gospel than by fear for his own life. He reminds us that we do not have much choice about how we will die; however, we have a lot of choice about how we shall live.

Brother Juniper (I)
d. 1258

"Would to God, my brothers, I had a whole forest of such Junipers," said Francis of this holy friar.

We don't know much about Juniper before he joined the friars in 1210. Francis sent him to establish "places" for the friars in Gualdo Tadino and Viterbo. When Saint Clare was dying, Juniper consoled her. He was devoted to the passion of Jesus and was known for his simplicity.

Several stories about Juniper in the *Little Flowers of St. Francis* illustrate his exasperating generosity. Once Juniper was taking care of a sick man who had a craving to eat pig's feet. This helpful friar went to a nearby field, captured a pig and cut off one foot, and then served this meal to the sick man. The owner of the pig was furious and immediately went to Juniper's superior. When Juniper saw his mistake, he apologized profusely. He also ended up talking this angry man into donating the rest of the pig to the friars!

Another time Juniper had been commanded to quit giving part of his clothing to the half-naked people he met on the road. Desiring to obey his superior, Juniper once told a man in need that he couldn't give the man his tunic, but he wouldn't prevent the man from taking it either. In time, the friars learned not to leave anything lying around, for Juniper would probably give it away.

He died in 1258 and is buried at Ara Coeli Church in Rome.

Quote: It is said that Saint Francis once described the perfect friar by citing "the patience of Brother Juniper, who attained the state of perfect patience because he kept the truth of his low estate constantly in mind, whose supreme desire was to follow Christ on the way of the cross" (*Mirror of Perfection*, #85).

Comment: What can we make of Juniper? He certainly seems to be the first of many Franciscan "characters." No doubt some of the stories about him have improved considerably in the retelling. Although the stories about Juniper may seem a little quaint, his virtues were not. He was humble because he knew the truth about God, himself and others. He was patient because he was willing to suffer ("patience" comes from *patior* meaning "to suffer") in his following of Jesus.

Saint Hyacintha of Mariscotti (III)
1585-1640

Hyacintha accepted God's standards somewhat late in life. Born of a noble family near Viterbo, she entered a local convent of sisters who followed the Third Order Rule. However, she supplied herself with enough food, clothing and other goods to live a very comfortable life amid these sisters pledged to mortification.

A serious illness required that Hyacintha's confessor bring Holy Communion to her room. Scandalized on seeing how soft a life she had provided for herself, the confessor advised her to live more humbly. Hyacintha disposed of her fine clothes and special foods. She eventually became very penitential in food and clothing; she was ready to do the most humble work in the convent. She developed a special devotion to the sufferings of Christ and by her penances became an inspiration to the sisters in her convent.

She was canonized in 1807.

Quote: Francis told his friars: "Blessed is the servant who would accept correction, accusation, and blame from another as patiently as he would from himself. Blessed is the servant who when he is rebuked quietly agrees, respectfully submits, humbly admits his fault, and willingly makes amends" (*Admonition XXII*).

Comment: How differently might Hyacintha's life have ended if her confessor had been afraid to question her pursuit of a soft life! Or what if she had refused to accept any challenge to her comfortable pattern of life? Francis of Assisi expected give and take in fraternal correction among his followers. Humility is required both of the one giving it and of the one receiving the correction; their roles could easily be reversed in the future. Such correction is really an act of charity and should be viewed that way by all concerned.

Blessed Veridiana of Castel Fiorentino (III)
1182-1242

Shortly before Saint Francis sought Pope Innocent III's verbal approval of the new brotherhood, Veridiana made a radical decision about how she would serve God.

Veridiana was born at Castel Fiorentino near Florence to the noble but poor Attavanti family. When she was twelve, she left home and began to help run her aunt's household. When a famine struck, Veridiana's generosity to the poor led her into trouble. She gave away some beans her uncle had already sold, making him very angry. A day later the storage bins were mysteriously refilled.

At the age of twenty-six, she decided to spend the rest of her life in prayer and penance. She became an anchoress; that is, she lived in a cell attached to the chapel of Saint Anthony in Florence. The cell had no doors — only a window for access to Holy Communion and the little food she needed.

In 1222 when Saint Francis was preaching near Florence, he gave Veridiana the habit of the Secular Franciscan Order and encouraged her life of contemplation. She died at prayer in her cell on February 1, 1242. The cell is preserved to this day.

Devotion to her was approved by Pope Clement VII in 1533.

Quote: In the Rule of 1221, Saint Francis wrote: "And whenever it may please them, all my brothers can proclaim this or a like exhortation and praise among all the people with the blessing of God: Fear and honor, praise and bless, give thanks and adore the Lord God Almighty in Trinity and in Unity, the Father and the Son and the Holy Spirit the Creator of all. Do penance, performing worthy fruits of penance since we will soon die. Give and it shall be given to you. Forgive and you shall be forgiven. And if you do not forgive men their sins, the Lord will not forgive you your sins. Confess all your sins" (Chapter 21).

Comment: One of the ironies of life is the fear that repentance and forgiveness somehow make us less human. In fact, they help us become more human — that is, more the men and women God intended us to be. Veridiana's thirty-four years as an anchoress may seem very peculiar; her prayerfulness and generosity to others were not.

Mother Alexia Hoell (III)
1838-1918

A generous response to the needs of God's people led Mother Alexia from Germany to the United States to establish a group of sisters. She later visited Europe to establish her sisters in new works of charity there.

Emma Franziska Hoell was the second of five children born to Dorothea Fritz and her husband, Anselm Hoell, in Buhlertal, Germany. Even as a child, Emma was generous in helping others.

When she was nineteen, Emma went to the Black Forest village of Schwarzach to join five other young women in caring for orphans under the direction of the parish priest. The women soon formed a religious congregation following the Franciscan Rule. Since the number of orphans increased more rapidly than did the money to care for them, Sister Alexia wanted some of her sisters to work in other jobs to support the work with the orphans. Their priest-founder, however, did not want a large group and because of financial necessity turned away some prospective sisters. By 1872 the group still had only ten members.

In that year, a wave of anti-Catholicism led the local archbishop to dispense the Schwarzach sisters from their vows and to allow them to return home. Sister Alexia saw this as a chance to establish the kind of self-supporting religious community she envisioned. With Sisters Alfons and Clara, she left for America.

Settling in Milwaukee, the sisters met Father Anton Michels, pastor of a rural parish seeking teachers for the local school. On April 28, 1874, the three sisters went to New Cassel (now Campbellsport), Wisconsin, to staff the parish school and to open a boarding school for girls. Their congregation, the School Sisters of St. Francis, was born.

Before the end of the century, these sisters had also started hospitals in the United States and had founded a European province which set up homes for delinquent young people and criminals, sanatoriums, orphanages, residences for young women students and several other socially-oriented activities.

Mother Alexia tended to select society's outcasts and the abandoned as her clientele. Even the official Church was not in favor of higher education for women when Mother Alexia began to promote it. The cofoundress, Mother Alfons, later said of Mother Alexia, "Hers was an extraordinary, lively, deeply social perception. Where want and need showed themselves, she brought help and alleviation."

Quote: Mother Alexia used to say "The needs of the time are the will of God."

Comment: Christ's Church still needs people with extraordinary compassion to show the face of Christ to the needy people in the world. The difference between the saints and many other people is not that the saints were more perceptive than anyone else but that the saints took risks where others decided to "play it safe."

Saint Joseph of Leonissa (I)
1556-1612

Joseph avoided the safe compromises by which people sometimes undercut the gospel. Born at Leonissa in the Kingdom of Naples, Joseph joined the Capuchins in his hometown in 1573. Denying himself hearty meals and comfortable quarters, he prepared for ordination and a life of preaching.

In 1587 he went to Constantinople to take care of the Christian galley slaves working under Turkish masters. Imprisoned for this work, he was warned not to resume it on his release. He did and was again imprisoned and then condemned to death. Miraculously freed, he returned to Italy where he preached to the poor and reconciled feuding families as well as warring cities which had been at odds for years. He was canonized in 1746.

Quote: In one of his sermons, Joseph says: "Every Christian must be a living book wherein one can read the teaching of the gospel. This is what Saint Paul says to the Corinthians, 'Clearly you are a letter of Christ which I have delivered, a letter written not with ink, but by the Spirit of the living God, not on tablets of stone but on tablets of flesh in the heart' (2 Corinthians 3:3). Our heart is the parchment; through my ministry the Holy Spirit is the writer because 'my tongue is like the pen of a ready scribe' (Psalm 45:1)."

Comment: Saints often jar us because they challenge our ideas about what we need for "the good life." "I'll be happy when. . . ," we may say, wasting an incredible amount of time on the periphery of life. People like Joseph of

---

18

Leonissa challenge us to face life courageously and get to the heart of it: life with God. Joseph was a compelling preacher because his life was as convincing as his words.

Mother Maria Theresia Bonzel (III)
1830-1905

Persecution of the Catholic Church in Germany enriched the Catholic Church in the United States. Opposition in one place can create the opportunity to serve God's people somewhere else. Like Saint Francis, Mother Theresia seized the opportunity instead of bewailing the loss.

Aline Bonzel was born in Olpe, a town in the southern part of Westfalen, Germany. She grew up in an affluent but deeply religious family. As a young woman she joined the Secular Franciscans.

The cross was familiar to Aline, whose father died when she was seven. In her teen years, heart trouble curtailed the sports she enjoyed. After Aline made her debut in society, she announced her desire to enter religious life, but Mrs. Bonzel refused her consent.

In 1859 Aline, her childhood friend, Regina Loeser, and a teacher, Klara Pfaender, began a new religious community in Olpe and dedicated themselves to contemplation, adoration of the Eucharist and the care of orphans.

When the teacher decided to base this new community on the Rule of Saint Augustine, Aline and her friend were troubled, for all three had at first agreed to follow the Rule of Saint Francis. The group separated into two communities in 1863 and Bishop Martin of Paderborn declared Olpe an independent religious community under the direction of Aline (now Mother Maria Theresia). The new community identified itself as the Sisters of Saint Francis of Perpetual Adoration.

Twelve years later the *Kulturkampf* (a Prussian-inspired anti-Catholic campaign) forbade the reception of new members into the community. That same year six sisters under the leadership of Sister Mary Clara Thomas came to the United States where the congregation grew rapidly. Schools, hospitals and orphanages were opened in the Midwest, the Louisiana delta, Arizona and New Mexico. The U.S. provinces are now headquartered in Mishawaka, Indiana, and in Colorado Springs, Colorado.

Mother Theresia cherished two great desires: to send her sisters to foreign missions and to have a small group of sisters devoted to the contem-

---

plative life. Today both wishes are a reality. A mission in the Philippines became Immaculate Conception Province in 1993. The German provinces staff missions in Brazil. Both in Germany and in the United States, a few contemplative sisters support the active apostolate with their life of prayer and penance.

Quote: Mother Maria Theresia sought God's will all her life. Her motto was "He leads; I follow."

Comment: Mother Maria Theresia's greatness is threefold. Her exterior apostolate was nourished in a rich life of prayer, especially adoration of our Lord in the Eucharist. She keenly understood the needs of her day and how the Church might address them. Her sisters engaged in apostolates far ahead of the conventions of the day: assisting mothers in labor, housing and caring for unwed mothers and working in half-way houses. As a humble, simple Franciscan, she treasured the little joys of everyday life just as gratefully as her ambitious plans.

February 6

Saint Peter Baptist and Companions (I, III)
d. 1597

Nagasaki is famous to us because of the atomic bomb exploded there in 1945. That city is also known among Franciscans for the friars and tertiaries martyred there in 1597.

Peter Baptist Blasquez was born in 1542 to a noble Spanish family; he joined the Franciscans in his homeland. He worked for several years in the Philippine Islands and in 1592 was delegated by Philip II of Spain to negotiate peace with Hideyoshi, the ruler of Japan.

Peter Baptist and several confreres accomplished their mission and stayed in Japan to spread the gospel. Their success in making converts and establishing churches and hospitals frightened Hideyoshi. In December, 1596, he imprisoned Peter Baptist, two other priests, two brothers, a cleric, seventeen Japanese Secular Franciscans and three Jesuits.

Condemned to death in early January at Miyako, these prisoners were led on a painful four-week trip to Nagasaki. On February 5, 1597, they were crucified and run through with spears. They were canonized in 1862.

Quote: Three days before his death, Peter Baptist wrote his confreres outside Japan: "For the love of God let your charity commend us to God that the sacrifice of our lives may be acceptable in his sight. From what I have heard here I think we will be crucified this coming Friday because it was on a Friday that they cut off a part of each one's ear at Miyako, an event we accept as a gift from God. We all ask you then with great fervor to pray for us for the love of God."

Comment: The "sacrifice" Peter Baptist referred to bore fruit. In the 1860's, Christian missionaries were again allowed into Nagasaki and found there a small but strong Catholic community which had begun in the time of the Franciscan martyrs. Coming together regularly, these Catholics read the Scriptures and prayed the rosary as a way of keeping their faith alive. Missionaries always work with trust that God will complete their beginnings. A good work — in the missions or elsewhere — is never wasted.

February 7

Saint Colette (II)
1381-1447

Colette did not seek the limelight, but in doing God's will she certainly attracted a lot of attention.

Colette was born in Corbie, France. At twenty-one she began to follow the Third Order Rule and became an anchoress, a woman walled into a room whose only opening was a window into a church.

After four years of prayer and penance in this cell, she left it. With the approval and encouragement of the pope, she joined the Poor Clares and reintroduced the primitive Rule of Saint Clare in the seventeen monasteries she established. Her sisters were known for their poverty — they rejected any fixed income — and for their perpetual fast. Colette's reform movement spread to other countries and is still thriving today. Colette was canonized in 1807.

Quote: In her spiritual testament, Colette told her sisters: "We must faithfully keep what we have promised. If through human weakness we fail, we must always without delay arise again by means of holy penance, and give our attention to leading a good life and to dying a holy death. May the

Father of all mercy, the Son by his holy passion, and the Holy Spirit, source of peace, sweetness and love, fill us with their consolation. Amen."

Comment: Colette began her reform during the time of the Great Western Schism (1378-1417) when three men claimed to be pope and thus divided Western Christianity. The fifteenth century in general was a very difficult one for the Western Church. Abuses long neglected cost the Church dearly in the following century; the prayers of Colette and her followers may have lessened the Church's troubles in the sixteenth century. In any case, Colette's reform indicated the entire Church's need to follow Christ more closely.

February 8

Saint Giles Mary of St. Joseph (I)
1729-1812

In the same year that a power-hungry Napoleon Bonaparte led his army into Russia, Giles Mary of St. Joseph ended a life of humble service to his Franciscan community and to the citizens of Naples.

Francesco was born in Taranto to very poor parents. His father's death left the eighteen-year-old Francesco to care for the family. Having secured their future, he entered the Friars Minor at Galatone in 1754. For fifty-three years he served as St. Paschal's Hospice in Naples in various roles, such as cook, porter or most often as official beggar for that community.

"Love God, love God" was his characteristic phrase as he gathered food for the friars and shared some of his bounty with the poor — all the while consoling the troubled and urging everyone to repent. The charity which he reflected on the streets of Naples was born in prayer and nurtured in the common life of the friars. The people whom Giles met on his begging rounds nicknamed him the "Consoler of Naples." He was canonized in 1996.

Quote: In his homily at the canonization of Giles, Pope John Paul II said that the spiritual journey of Giles reflected "the humility of the Incarnation and the gratuitousness of the Eucharist" (1996 LOR 23:1).

Comment: People often become arrogant and power hungry when they try to live a lie, for example, when they forget their own sinfulness and ignore the gifts God has given to other people. Giles had a healthy sense of his own sinfulness — not paralyzing but not superficial either. He invited men and women to recognize their own gifts and to live out their dignity as people made in God's divine image. Knowing someone like Giles can help us on our own spiritual journey.

Saint Conrad of Piacenza (III)
1290-1350

Born of a noble family in northern Italy, Conrad as a young man married Euphrosyne, daughter of a nobleman.

One day while hunting he ordered attendants to set fire to some brush in order to flush out the game. The fire spread to nearby fields and to a large forest. Conrad fled. An innocent peasant was imprisoned, tortured to confess and condemned to death. Conrad confessed his guilt, saved the man's life and paid for the damaged property.

Soon after this event, Conrad and his wife agreed to separate: she to a Poor Clare monastery and he to a group of hermits following the Third Order Rule. His reputation for holiness, however, spread quickly. Since his many visitors destroyed his solitude, Conrad went to a more remote spot in Sicily where he lived thirty-six years as a hermit, praying for himself and for the rest of the world.

Prayer and penance were his answer to the temptations that beset him. Conrad died kneeling before a crucifix. He was canonized in 1625.

Quote: Pope Paul VI's 1969 *Instruction on the Contemplative Life* includes this passage: "To withdraw into the desert is for Christians tantamount to associating themselves more intimately with Christ's passion, and it enables them, in a very special way, to share in the paschal mystery and in the passage of Our Lord from this world to the heavenly homeland" (#1).

Comment: Francis of Assisi was drawn both to contemplation and to a life of preaching; periods of intense prayer nourished his preaching. Some of his early followers, however, felt called to a life of greater contemplation, and he accepted that. Though Conrad of Piacenza is not the norm in the Church, he and other contemplatives remind us of the greatness of God and of the joys of heaven.

Blessed Sebastian of Aparicio (I)
1502-1600

Sebastian's roads and bridges connected many distant places. His final bridge-building was to help men and women recognize their God-given dignity and destiny.

Sebastian's parents were Spanish peasants. At the age of thirty-one he sailed to Mexico, where he began working in the fields. Eventually he built roads to facilitate agricultural trading and other commerce. His 466-mile road from Mexico City to Zacatecas took ten years to build and required careful negotiations with the indigenous peoples along the way.

In time Sebastian was a wealthy farmer and rancher. At the age of sixty he entered a virginal marriage. His wife's motivation may have been a large inheritance; his was to provide a respectable life for a girl without even a modest marriage dowry. When his first wife died, he entered another virginal marriage for the same reason; his second wife also died young.

At the age of seventy-two Sebastian distributed his goods among the poor and entered the Franciscans as a brother. Assigned to the large (100-member) friary at Puebla de los Angeles south of Mexico City, Sebastian went out collecting alms for the friars for the next twenty-five years. His charity to all earned him the nickname "Angel of Mexico."

Sebastian was beatified in 1787 and is known as a patron of travelers.

Quote: Saint Francis once told his followers: "There is a contract between the world and the friars. The friars must give the world a good example; the world must provide for their needs. When they break faith and withdraw their good example, the world will withdraw its hand in a just censure" (2 *Celano*, #70).

Comment: According to the Rule of Saint Francis, the friars were to work for their daily bread. Sometimes, however, their work would not provide for their needs; for example, working with people suffering from leprosy brought little or no pay. In cases such as these, the friars were allowed to beg, always keeping in mind the admonition of Francis to let their good example commend them to the people. The life of the prayerful Sebastian, still hard at work in his nineties, certainly drew many closer to God.

Saint Agnes of Bohemia (II)
1205-1282

Agnes had no children of her own but was certainly life-giving for all who knew her.

Agnes was the daughter of Queen Constance and King Ottokar I of Bohemia. At the age of three, she was betrothed to the Duke of Silesia, who died three years later. As she grew up, she decided she wanted to enter the religious life.

After declining marriages to King Henry VII of Germany and Henry III of England, Agnes was faced with a proposal from Frederick II, the Holy Roman Emperor. She appealed to Pope Gregory IX for help. The pope was persuasive; Frederick magnanimously said that he could not be offended if Agnes preferred the King of Heaven to him.

After Agnes built a hospital for the poor and a residence for the friars, she financed the construction of a Poor Clare monastery in Prague. In 1236, she and seven other noblewomen entered this monastery. Saint Clare sent five sisters from San Damiano to join them, and wrote Agnes four letters advising her on the beauty of her vocation and her duties as abbess.

Agnes became known for prayer, obedience and mortification. Papal pressure forced her to accept her election as abbess; nevertheless, the title she preferred was "senior sister." Her position did not prevent her from cooking for the other sisters and mending the clothes of lepers. The sisters found her kind but very strict regarding the observance of poverty; she declined her royal brother's offer to set up an endowment for the monastery.

Devotion to Agnes arose soon after her death on March 6, 1282. She was canonized in 1989.

Quote: "Have nothing to do with anyone who would stand in your way and would seek to turn you aside from fulfilling the vows which you have made to the Most High (Psalm 49:14) and from living in that perfection to which the Spirit of the Lord has called you" (Clare to Agnes, *Letter II* in Murray Bodo, O.F.M., *Clare: A Light in the Garden*, page 118).

Comment: Agnes spent at least forty-five years in a Poor Clare monastery. Such a life requires a great deal of patience and charity. The temptation to selfishness certainly didn't vanish when Agnes walked into the monastery. It is perhaps easy for us to think that cloistered nuns "have it made" regarding holiness. Their route is the same as ours: gradual exchange of our standards (inclination to selfishness) for God's standard of generosity.

March 3

Blessed Liberatus Weiss, Samuele Marzorati and Michele Pio Fasoli (I)
d. 1716

These three friars died together as martyrs after having worked to promote unity between Ethiopian Christians and Christians of the Latin Rite.

Liberatus (b. 1675 in Bavaria) entered the Friars Minor in Vienna. In 1703 he left for Ethiopia and was named Prefect Apostolic there in 1711. Samuele (b. 1670 in Varese) joined the Order in Milano and studied medicine in Rome in preparation for his missionary work. Michele was born in Pavia, joined the Piemonte province and received an obedience for Ethiopia in 1704.

In 1698, the Congregation for the Propagation of the Faith had entrusted the kingdoms of Ahmin (Egypt) and Fungi (Ethiopia) to the spiritual care of the Friars Minor. Liberatus and Michele had worked in Egypt for several years before entering Ethiopia with Samuele in 1711. They went at the invitation of Emperor Justos, who like Pope Clement XI, sought to unite the two churches. Once the friars had entered Ethiopia, however, the emperor forbade them to preach; he was overthrown in 1715.

On March 3, 1716, these three friars were stoned to death in Gondar because they would not deny the two natures of Christ and refused to accept certain customs of the Ethiopian Church. In his homily at their 1988 beatification, Pope John Paul II described the martyrdom of Liberatus, Samuele and Michele as the supreme act of a strong love and a tenacious faith.

Quote: Archbishop Desmond Tutu once told a group of Anglican deacons: "When we have done our best in our sermons, in our teaching, in whatever we do, then success or failure are for God to determine, and after all, God's ways are not our ways and it is always He who gives the increase. Success and failure are not as the world understands these things. But we must be faithful. This is where discipline comes in" (*Hope and Suffering*, page 72).

Comment: At their beatification, Pope John Paul II said that the martyrdom of Liberatus, Samuele and Michele recalls a time when relations between these sister churches were marked by mutual misunderstandings of each other's language and culture. We must be disciplined in our dialogue with other Christians as well as in our preaching. In all things, it is "only God who gives the growth" (1 Corinthians 3:7).

March 5

Saint John Joseph of the Cross (I)
1654-1734

Self-denial is never an end in itself but is only a help toward greater charity — as the life of Saint John Joseph shows.

John Joseph was very ascetic even as a young man. At sixteen he joined the Franciscans in Naples; he was the first Italian to follow the reform movement of Saint Peter Alcantara (October 22). John's reputation for holiness prompted his superiors to put him in charge of establishing a new friary even before he was ordained.

Obedience moved John to accept appointments as novice master, guardian and, finally, provincial. His years of mortification enabled him to offer these services to the friars with great charity. As guardian he was not above working in the kitchen or carrying the wood and water needed by the friars.

When his term as provincial expired, John Joseph dedicated himself to hearing confessions and practicing mortification, two concerns contrary to the spirit of the dawning Age of Enlightenment. John Joseph was canonized in 1839.

Quote: "And by this I wish to know if you love the Lord God and me, his servant and yours — if you have acted in this manner: that is, there should not be any brother in the world who has sinned, however much he may have possibly sinned, who, after he has looked into your eyes, would go away without having received your mercy, if he is looking for mercy. And if he were not to seek mercy, you should ask him if he wants mercy. And if he should sin thereafter a thousand times before your very eyes, love him more than me so that you may draw him back to the Lord. Always be merciful to [brothers] such as these" (Saint Francis, *Letter to a Minister*).

Comment: John Joseph's mortification allowed him to be the kind of forgiving superior intended by Saint Francis. Self-denial should lead us to charity—not to bitterness; it should help us clarify our priorities and make us more loving. John Joseph is living proof of Chesterton's observation: "It is always easy to let the age have its head; the difficult thing is to keep one's own" (G. K. Chesterton, *Orthodoxy*, page 101).

March 12

Blessed Angela Salawa (III)
1881-1922

Angela served Christ and Christ's little ones with all her strength. Born in Siepraw, near Kraków, she was the eleventh child of Bartlomiej and Ewa Salawa. In 1897, she moved to Kraków where her older sister Therese lived. Angela immediately began to gather together and instruct young women domestic workers. During World War I, she helped prisoners of war without regard for their nationality or religion. The writings of Teresa of Avila and John of the Cross were a great comfort to her.

Angela gave great service in caring for soldiers wounded in World War I. After 1918 her health did not permit her to exercise her customary apostolate. Addressing herself to Christ, she wrote in her diary, "I want you to be adored as much as you were destroyed." In another place, she wrote, "Lord, I live by your will. I shall die when you desire; save me because you can."

At her 1991 beatification in Kraków, Pope John Paul II said: "It is in this city that she worked, that she suffered and that her holiness came to maturity. While connected to the spirituality of Saint Francis, she showed an extraordinary responsiveness to the action of the Holy Spirit" (1991 LOR 34:4).

Quote: Henri de Lubac, S.J., wrote: "The best Christians and the most vital are by no means to be found either inevitably or even generally among the wise or the clever, the intelligentsia or the politically-minded, or those of social consequence. And consequently what they say does not make the headlines; what they do does not come to the public eye. Their lives are hidden from the eyes of the world, and if they do come to some degree of notoriety, that is usually late in the day, and exceptional, and always attended by the risk of distortion" (*The Splendor of the Church*, page 187).

Comment: Humility should never be mistaken for lack of conviction, insight or energy. Angela brought the Good News and material assistance to some of Christ's "least ones." Her self-sacrifice inspired others to do the same.

March 18

Saint Salvator of Horta (I)
1520-1567

A reputation for holiness does have some drawbacks. Public recognition can be a nuisance at times — as the confreres of Salvator found out.

Salvator was born during Spain's Golden Age. Art, politics and wealth were flourishing. So was religion. Ignatius of Loyola founded the Society of Jesus in 1540.

Salvator's parents were poor. At the age of twenty-one, he entered the Franciscans as a brother and was soon known for his asceticism, humility and simplicity.

As cook, porter and later the official beggar for the friars in Tortosa, he became well known for his charity. He healed the sick with the Sign of the Cross. When crowds of sick people began coming to the friary to see Salvator, the friars transferred him to Horta. Again the sick flocked to ask his intercession; one person estimated that two thousand people a week came to see Salvator. He told them to examine their consciences, to go to confession and to receive Holy Communion worthily. He refused to pray for those who would not receive those sacraments.

The public attention given to Salvator was relentless. The crowds would sometimes tear off pieces of his habit as relics. Two years before his death, Salvator was moved again, this time to Cagliari on the island of Sardinia. He died at Cagliari saying, "Into your hands, O Lord, I commend my spirit." He was canonized in 1938.

Quote: "Then Jesus summoned his twelve disciples and gave them authority over unclean spirits, to cast them out, and to cure every disease and every sickness" (Matthew 10:1).

Comment: Medical science is now seeing more clearly the relation of some diseases to one's emotional and spiritual life. In *Healing Life's Hurts*, Matthew and Dennis Linn report that sometimes people experience relief from illness only when they have decided to forgive others. Salvator prayed that people might be healed, and many were. Surely not all diseases can be treated this way; medical help should not be abandoned. But notice that Salvator urged his petitioners to reestablish their priorities in life before they asked for healing.

March 22

Saint Benvenute of Osimo (I)
d. 1282

The spirit of Saint Francis can be found among bishops.

Benvenute came from the prominent Scotivoli family in Ancona, Italy. After studying theology and law at the University of Bologna, he was ordained and sent back to Ancona to assist in the running of the diocese.

Then he was appointed administrator of the Diocese of Osimo. That city had been without a bishop for twenty years as punishment for siding with Emperor Frederick II in his wars against the pope. Benvenute succeeded in convincing the people of Osimo to return to obedience to the pope. In 1264 the pope named Benvenute Bishop of Osimo, but allowed him to become a Franciscan before taking up his episcopal duties.

As a bishop Benvenute wore the Franciscan habit and observed the Rule of Saint Francis carefully. He promoted reform in his diocese by calling together synods and establishing wise rules to combat existing abuses. In all, Benvenute led the men and women of his diocese closer to God.

He died in his cathedral amid his priests. He was canonized three years later.

Quote: "In exercising their office of fathers and pastors, bishops should be with their people as those who serve, as good shepherds who know their sheep and whose sheep know them, as true fathers who excel in their love and solicitude for all, to whose divinely conferred authority all readily submit. They should so unite and mold their flock into one family that all, conscious of their duties, may live and act as one in charity" (Vatican II, *Decree on the Pastoral Office of Bishops*, #16).

Comment: People from all walks of life have followed Christ after the example of Saint Francis. While most Franciscan bishops have served in the missions, there have been a significant number like Benvenute. Positions of leadership have made these bishops even more aware that humility and poverty are the marks of Christ's Church.

March 23

Saint Catherine of Genoa (III)
1447-1510

Going to confession one day was the turning point of Catherine's life. When Catherine was born, many Italian nobles were supporting Renaissance artists and writers. The needs of the poor and the sick were often overshadowed by a hunger for luxury and self-indulgence.

Catherine's parents were members of the nobility in Genoa. At thirteen she attempted to become a nun but failed because of her age. At sixteen she married Julian, a nobleman who turned out to be selfish and unfaithful. For a while she tried to numb her disappointment by a life of selfish pleasure.

One day in confession she had a new sense of her own sins and how much God loved her. She reformed her life and gave good example to Julian, who soon turned from his self-centered life of distraction.

Julian's spending, however, had ruined them financially. He and Catherine decided to live in the Pammatone, a large hospital in Genoa, and to dedicate themselves to works of charity there. After Julian's death in 1497, Catherine took over management of the hospital.

She wrote about purgatory which, she said, begins on earth for souls open to God. Life with God in heaven is a continuation and perfection of the life with God begun on earth.

Exhausted by her life of self-sacrifice, she died September 15, 1510, and was canonized in 1737.

Quote: Shortly before Catherine's death she told her goddaughter: "Tomasina! Jesus in your heart! Eternity in your mind! The will of God in all your actions! But above all, love, God's love, entire love!" (Marion A. Habig, O.F.M., *The Franciscan Book of Saints*, page 212).

Comment: Regular confessions and frequent Communion can help us see the direction (or drift) of our life with God. People who have a realistic sense of their own sinfulness and of the greatness of God are often the ones who are most ready to meet the needs of their neighbors. Catherine began her hospital work with enthusiasm and was faithful to it through difficult times because she was inspired by the love of God, a love which was renewed in her by the Scriptures and the sacraments.

March 29

Blessed Ludovico of Casoria (I)
1814-1885

Born in Casoria (near Naples), Arcangelo Palmentieri was a cabinet-maker before entering the Friars Minor in 1832, taking the name Ludovico. After his ordination five years later, he taught chemistry, physics and mathematics to younger members of his province for several years.

In 1847 he had a mystical experience which he later described as a cleansing. After that he dedicated his life to the poor and the infirm, establishing a dispensary for the poor, two schools for African children, an institute for the children of nobility, as well as an institution for orphans, the deaf and the speechless, and other institutes for the blind, elderly and for travelers. In addition to an infirmary for friars of his province, he began charitable institutes in Naples, Florence and Assisi. He once said, "Christ's love has wounded my heart." This love prompted him to great acts of charity.

To help continue these works of mercy, in 1859 he established the Gray Brothers, a religious community composed of men who formerly belonged to the Secular Franciscan Order. Three years later he founded the Gray Sisters of St. Elizabeth for the same purpose.

Toward the beginning of his final, nine-year illness, Ludovico wrote a spiritual testament which described faith as "light in the darkness, help in sickness, blessing in tribulations, paradise in the crucifixion and life amid death." The local work for his beatification began within five months of Ludovico's death. He was beatified in 1993.

Quote: Ludovico's spiritual testament begins: "The Lord called me to himself with a most tender love, and with an infinite charity he led and directed me along the path of my life."

Comment: Saintly people are not protected from suffering, but with God's help they learn how to develop compassion from it. In the face of great suffering, we move either toward compassion or indifference. Saintly men and women show us the path toward compassion.

March 30

Saint Peter Regaldo (I)
1390-1456

Peter lived at a very busy time. The Great Western Schism (1378-1417) was settled at the Council of Constance (1414-1418). France and England were fighting the Hundred Years' War, and in 1453 the Byzantine Empire was completely wiped out by the loss of Constantinople to the Turks. At Peter's death the age of printing had just begun in Germany, and the discovery of America was less than forty years away.

Peter came from a wealthy and pious family in Vallodolid, Spain. At the age of thirteen, he was allowed to enter the Conventual Franciscans. Shortly after his ordination, he was made superior of the friary in Aguilar. He became part of a group of friars who wanted to lead a life of greater poverty and penance. In 1442 he was appointed head of all the Spanish Franciscans in his reform group.

Peter led the friars by his example. A special love of the poor and the sick characterized Peter. Miraculous stories are told about his charity to the poor. For example, the bread never seemed to run out as long as Peter had hungry people to feed. Throughout most of his life, Peter went hungry; he lived only on bread and water.

Immediately after his death on March 31, 1456, his grave became a place of pilgrimage. Peter was canonized in 1746.

Quote: "And let all the brothers, both the ministers and servants as well as the others, take care not to be disturbed or angered at the sin or the evil of another, because the devil wishes to destroy many through the fault of one; but they should spiritually help [the brother] who has sinned as best they can, because it is not the healthy who are in need of the physician, but whose who are sick (cf. Mt 9:12; Mk 2:17)" (*Rule of 1221*, Chapter 5).

Comment: Peter was an effective leader of the friars because he did not become ensnared in anger over the sins of others. Peter helped sinning friars rearrange the priorities in their lives and dedicate themselves to living the gospel of Jesus Christ as they had vowed. This patient correction is an act of charity available to all Franciscans, not just to superiors.

April 2

Blessed Elisabetta Vendramini (III)
1790-1860

"The love of Christ urges us on" (2 Corinthians 5:14) was Elisabetta's guiding star.

Born in Bassano del Grappa near Treviso, at age twenty-seven Elisabetta broke off an engagement to marry and decided to alleviate the moral and material sufferings of the poor. She began working at a girls' orphanage in her hometown in 1820 and joined the Secular Franciscan Order the following year. After moving to Padua in 1828, she continued working with children. In 1830 she founded the Franciscan Tertiary Sisters of Saint Elizabeth of Hungary. Until her death Elisabetta guided this community, which dedicated itself to teaching as well as caring for the elderly, orphans and the sick. She united her physical sufferings with those of Christ and the Sorrowful Mother Mary. Elisabetta was beatified in 1990.

Quote: During his homily for her beatification, Pope John Paul II said that from her prayer Elisabetta drew "the dynamism of the Incarnation of the Word, in order to give praise and admiration to the Poor and Crucified Christ, whom she recognized and served in her beloved poor." Later he pointed out: "Blessed Elisabetta teaches us that wherever faith is strong and sure, our charitable outreach to our neighbor will be more daring. Wherever our sense of Christ is more acute, our sense of the needs of our brothers and sisters will be more correct and on target" (1990 LOR 46:1).

Comment: Saintly people show us that love of God and love of neighbor are two sides of the same coin. Love of God strengthens us as we take small but

---

concrete steps to express our love of neighbor. Our inability to do everything needed should not stop us from doing what we can.

April 3

Saint Benedict the African (I)
1526-1589

Benedict held important posts in the Order and gracefully adjusted to other work when his terms of office were up.

His parents were slaves brought from Africa to Messina, Sicily. Freed at eighteen, Benedict did farm work for a wage and soon saved enough to buy a pair of oxen. He was very proud of those animals. In time he joined a group of hermits around Palermo and was eventually recognized as their leader. Because these hermits followed the Rule of Saint Francis, Pope Pius IV ordered them to join the First Order.

Benedict was eventually novice master and then guardian of the friars in Palermo — positions rarely held in those days by a brother. In fact, Benedict was forced to accept his election as guardian. And when his term ended he happily returned to his work in the friary kitchen.

Benedict corrected the friars with humility and charity. Once he corrected a novice and assigned him a penance only to learn that the novice was not the guilty party. Benedict immediately knelt down before the novice and asked his pardon.

In later life Benedict was not possessive of the few things he used. He never referred to them as "mine" but always called them "ours." His gifts for prayer and the guidance of souls earned him throughout Sicily a reputation for holiness. Following the example of Saint Francis, Benedict kept seven forty-day fasts throughout the year; he also slept only a few hours each night.

After Benedict's death, King Philip III of Spain paid for a special tomb for this holy friar. Canonized in 1807, he is honored as a patron saint by African-Americans.

Quote: "I did not come to be served but to serve (cf. Mt 10:28), says the Lord. Those who are placed over others should glory in such an office only as much as they would were they assigned the task of washing the feet of the brothers. And the more they are upset about their office being taken from them than they would be over the loss of the office of [washing] feet, so much the more do they store up treasures to the peril of their souls (cf. Jn 12:6)" (Francis of Assisi, *Admonition IV*).

Comment: Among Franciscans a position of leadership is limited in time. When the time expires, former leaders sometimes have trouble adjusting to their new position. The Church needs men and women ready to put their best energies into leadership — but men and women who are gracefully willing to go on to other work when their time of leadership is over.

April 4

Leonard Foley (I)
1913-1994

F rancis of Assisi shared the Good News of Jesus with his words, deeds and songs. Leonard used pen, typewriter and computer to share that same Good News.

Born in Lafayette, Indiana, Leonard made his first profession in 1932. After his ordination eight years later, he taught English for eleven years at his province's minor seminary. Two years as an assistant pastor preceded many years of preaching retreats and parish missions.

In 1963 he began studying journalism in preparation for taking over as editor of *St. Anthony Messenger*. He launched a new era in the history of the magazine with the November 1964 issue, introducing columns for letters, books and movie reviews, as well as articles on contemporary social issues and the changes in the Church that followed Vatican II. He had a strong desire to communicate the richness of Vatican II's teachings to readers and listeners.

In all of his writings, he shared the Good News and God's incredibly patient love for all people. "Poor people, poor God," he sometimes said after encountering a person with an obviously religious temperament, but a poor self-image and an oppressive image of God. He helped many people to discover themselves, to believe in themselves and to know that God loves them. Leonard frequently spoke at parish Lenten or Advent programs, always aiming to explain things in terms that his favorite Aunt Mamie, a woman of deep but simple faith, would understand.

Leonard wrote *Catholic Updates* and books to foster adult education and to help people understand Vatican II. His popular book *Believing in Jesus: A Popular Overview of the Catholic Faith* has sold nearly half a million copies and continues to instruct and nourish people interested in learning more about Catholicism.

Leonard encouraged many people to explore their writing talents, showing them how to clarify their intent and sharpen their impact on readers. His constructive critiques and sober praise lightened the task of rewriting.

A man of faith, he confronted his final illness with courage and faith. Not long before his death he said to a friend, "Just remember, Patti, God is good and life is wonderful." His sense of humor never deserted him, and God welcomed him home on Easter Sunday morning in 1994.

Quote: Leonard wrote: "A loving God offers us friendship, and the result of that gracious act is our holiness.... Faith is the gift whereby we are able to receive a gift. We are able to open ourselves to God's friendship, communion, oneness. Our freedom becomes total freedom when we let Christ enfold it in his own.... [Saints] remind us that the Church is holy, can never stop being holy and is called to show the holiness of God by living the life of Christ. Our holiness is the same as theirs — God's holiness" (Leonard Foley, *Saint of the Day*, pages 2-3).

Comment: The images of God that we acquire early in life may need some reexamination later in life. Those images influence the way we see others and ourselves. Leonard exemplifies the holiness that results from growing honesty with God, with oneself and with others.

April 21

Saint Conrad of Parzham (I)
1818-1894

Conrad spent most of his life as porter in Altoetting, Bavaria, letting people into the friary and indirectly encouraging them to let God into their lives.

His parents, Bartholomew and Gertrude Birndorfer, lived near Parzham, Bavaria. In those days this region was recovering from the Napoleonic wars. A lover of solitary prayer and a peacemaker as a young man, Conrad joined the Capuchins as a brother. He made his profession in 1852 and was assigned to the friary in Altoetting. That city's shrine to

Mary was very popular; at the nearby Capuchin friary there was a lot of work for the porter, a job Conrad held for forty-one years.

At first some of the other friars were jealous that such a young friar held this important job. Conrad's patience and holy life overcame their doubts. As porter he dealt with many people, obtaining many of the friary supplies and generously providing for the poor who came to the door. He treated them all with the courtesy Francis expected of his followers.

Conrad's helpfulness was sometimes unnerving. Once Father Vincent, seeking quiet to prepare a sermon, went up the belltower of the church. Conrad tracked him down when someone wanting to go to confession specifically requested Father Vincent.

Conrad also developed a special rapport with the children of the area. He enthusiastically promoted the Seraphic Work of Charity, which aided neglected children.

Conrad spent hours in prayer before the Blessed Sacrament. He regularly asked the Blessed Mother to intercede for him and for the many people he included in his prayers. The ever-patient Conrad was canonized in 1934.

Quote: "It was God's will that I should leave everything that was near and dear to me. I thank him for having called me to religious life where I have found such peace and joy as I could never have found in the world. My plan of life is chiefly this: to love and suffer, always meditating upon, adoring and admiring God's unspeakable love for his lowliest creatures" (*Letter of Saint Conrad*).

Comment: As we can see from his life as well as his words, Conrad of Parzham lived a life that attracted others because of a special quality, something Chesterton alluded to when he wrote, "The moment we have a fixed heart we have a free hand" (*Orthodoxy*, page 71). If we want to understand Conrad, we have to know where he fixed his heart. Because he was united to God in prayer, everyone felt at ease in Conrad's presence.

Blessed Giles of Assisi (I)
1190-1262

Giles, one of the first followers of Saint Francis, was a simple and prayer-ful man.

Giles the farmer distributed his goods to the poor and became one of Francis' first disciples on April 23, 1208. The Poverello introduced Giles to the others saying, "Here is a good brother God has sent us! Let us sit down to table and celebrate his coming."

Early in his life as a Franciscan, Giles went on pilgrimages to Rome, to the Holy Land and to the famous shrine of Saint James at Compostela, Spain. His 1219 preaching mission to the Muslims of Tunis was cut short when Christians there, fearing he would cause trouble for them, put him on the boat back to Italy. Giles then worked several years as a day-laborer. In 1234 he moved to Monte Ripido near Perugia to pursue a contemplative life. Giles lived there until his death.

Giles always worked for his daily bread even if he was a guest someplace. Once when he was staying with a cardinal, the morning brought a hard rain. The cardinal happily thought that Giles would miss a day's work and have to accept his charity. The ingenious friar, however, went to the kitchen of the palace and spent the day helping the cook clean it and prepare the evening meal!

When Saint Bonaventure (July 15) came to Perugia, Giles asked him if an ignorant person could love God as much as a scholar. Bonaventure, one of the leading theologians from the University of Paris and at the time minister general of the friars, responded, "A little old woman can love God even more than a master of theology." Giles immediately ran out, met an old woman and told her, "O poor little old woman, though you are simple and uneducated, just love the Lord God and you can be greater than Brother Bonaventure."

Pope Gregory IX, the former Cardinal Hugolino and a great admirer of Saint Francis, once brought Giles to Viterbo in order to experience his holiness firsthand. They began speaking of heaven, and Giles twice went into ecstasy for long periods of time. The pope was convinced. Another time the pope asked Giles for some advice about fulfilling his duties as pope. Giles told him that he should have two eyes in his soul: one to contemplate heavenly things and the other to direct earthly things.

As the pope and Bonaventure agreed, Giles was a master of the spiritual life. *The Golden Sayings of Brother Giles* records some of his most memorable quotes.

One of the last of Francis' early followers to die, Giles denounced any relaxation of discipline in the Rule of Saint Francis. He was particularly worried that some of the young friars being educated at the University of Paris would develop the intellectual pride so foreign to Saint Francis. Giles was beatified in 1777.

Quote: "The birds of the air and the beasts of the earth and the fishes of the sea are satisfied when they have enough food for themselves. But since man is not satisfied with the things of this world and always longs for others, it is clear that he was not made primarily for them but for others. For the body was made for the sake of the soul, and this world for the sake of the other world" (*Golden Sayings*).

Comment: We are created for a purpose. Giles knew that our goal is life with God and happily prepared himself for it.

April 24

Saint Fidelis of Sigmaringen (I)
1578-1622

Fidelis gave up a profession he considered too dangerous and died a martyr!

Born when the Reformation had already taken firm root in Germany, the Netherlands, France and Switzerland, Fidelis came from a leading family in Sigmaringen, Germany. After receiving doctorates in philosophy and in law (canon and civil) at the University of Freiburg in Breisgau, he became a lawyer. When he saw how many lawyers were corrupted by greed, however, he began to fear for his soul and joined the Capuchins.

The superior's words to him at profession of vows, "Be faithful until death, and I will give you the crown of life" (Revelation 2:10), proved prophetic. After ordination Fidelis began a preaching career that was interrupted by his appointment as guardian at Feldkirch and in several other places. In one place Fidelis distinguished himself by nursing soldiers felled by an epidemic. Insisting on strict poverty, Fidelis was an inspiration to the friars.

In 1622, the newly established Congregation for the Propagation of the Faith (*Propaganda Fide*) named Fidelis to head a mission to the Calvinists in Switzerland. He converted a fair number of them. Killed while preaching in the church at Seewis, Fidelis is considered the first martyr of the Propaganda.

Fidelis, the patron of lawyers, was canonized in 1746.

Quote: "Action on behalf of justice and participation in the transformation of the world fully appear to us as a constitutive dimension of the preaching of the gospel or, in other words, of the Church's mission for the redemption of the human race and its liberation from every oppressive situation" (1971 Synod of Bishops, *Justice in the World*, Introduction).

Comment: Fidelis can inspire us in two ways: to work for justice on behalf of the poor and to work for the spread of the gospel of Jesus Christ. His reservation about practicing law was not shared by Saint Ivo of Brittany (May 10) or Saint Thomas More (June 22).

Fidelis used to pray that he might never be halfhearted in his service of Jesus; the same temptation is present for us. Working for justice is dangerous work and is sometimes mistakenly considered an "extra" in the following of Jesus. Without championing any one political party or system, the followers of Jesus must help all peoples realize their God-given dignity.

April 25

Blessed Pedro de San José Betancur (III)
1626-1667

Pedro very much wanted to become a priest, but God had other plans. Born of a poor family on Tenerife in the Canary Islands, Pedro was a shepherd until 1650 when he left for Guatemala, where he had a relative in government service. He got as far as Havana when his money ran out. After he had earned more money, he went on to Guatemala City in 1651. When he arrived he was so poor that he benefited from the breadline that the Franciscans had established.

Pedro enrolled in the local Jesuit college in hopes of studying for the priesthood. No matter how hard he tried, however, he could not make the studies and so had to withdraw. In 1655 he joined the Secular Franciscan Order. Three years later he opened a hospital for the convalescent poor; a shelter for the homeless and a school for the poor soon followed. Not wanting to neglect the rich of Guatemala City, Pedro began walking through their part of town ringing a bell and inviting them to repent.

Other men came to share in Pedro's work. Out of this group came the Bethlehemite Congregation, which won papal approval after Pedro's death.

He is sometimes credited with originating the Christmas Eve *posadas* procession in which people representing Mary and Joseph seek a night's lodging from their neighbors. The custom soon spread to Mexico and other Central American countries. Pedro was beatified in 1980.

Quote: Speaking of Pedro and the four others beatified with him, Pope John Paul II said: "God lavished his kindness and his mercy on them, enriching them with his grace; he loved them with a fatherly, but demanding, love, which promised only hardships and suffering. He invited and called them to heroic holiness; he tore them away from their countries of origin and sent them to other lands to proclaim the message of the gospel, in the midst of inexpressible toil and difficulties" (1980 LOR 26:10).

Comment: The life of any holy Christian reveals an inner dynamism to use one's best energies for the spread of the gospel. God's love is indeed "demanding." It calls for ever-expanding generosity such as Pedro had. Saints are simply people who, with God's grace, have tried to find the most generous way of living out God's love.

April 27

Saint Zita of Lucca (III)
1218-1278

Zita is a good saint for those of us who sometimes lose a chance to do some good by waiting to do something better.

Saint Francis of Assisi was still living when Zita was born to poor, devout Italian parents. From the age of twelve until her death, she worked as a servant for the Fatinelli family in Lucca. She was a hard worker, pious and generous. Although that dedication provoked jealousy on the part of some other servants, Zita won them over by her patience.

As the years passed, she became famous for helping the sick, the poor and the imprisoned. She was regarded locally as a saint soon after her death; that title was officially given to her in 1696. Zita is the patroness of domestic workers.

Quote: "Let us then have charity and humility; let us give alms since this washes our souls from the stains of [our] sins (cf. Tobit 4:11; 12:9). For people lose everything they leave behind in this world; but they carry with them the rewards of charity and the alms which they gave, for which they will have a reward and a suitable remuneration from the Lord" (Saint Francis, *Second Version of the Letter to the Faithful*).

Comment: "You can't take it with you," we say. Yet often people are afraid to perform the corporal works of mercy because they fear depleting their resources — time, money or energy. Zita is honored as a saint largely because of her charity. She might have compared herself with others having greater resources and excused herself from aiding Christ's poor. She lived out Jesus' story about the widow's mite (see Luke 21:1-4).

April 28

Blessed Luchesio and Buonadonna (III)
d. 1260

Luchesio and his wife Buonadonna wanted to follow Saint Francis as a married couple. Thus they set in motion the Secular Franciscan Order.

Luchesio and Buonadonna lived in Poggibonzi where he was a greedy merchant. Meeting Francis — probably in 1213 — changed his life. He began to perform many works of charity.

At first Buonadonna was not as enthusiastic about giving so much away as Luchesio was. One day after complaining that he was giving everything to strangers, Buonadonna answered the door only to find someone else needing help. Luchesio asked her to give the poor man some bread. She frowned but went to the pantry anyway. There she discovered more bread than had been there the last time she looked. She soon became as zealous for a poor and simple life as Luchesio was. They sold the business, farmed enough land to provide for their needs and distributed the rest to the poor.

In the thirteenth century some couples, by mutual consent and with the Church's permission, separated so that the husband could join a monastery (or a group such as Francis began) and his wife could go to a cloister. Conrad of Piacenza (February 19) and his wife did just that. This choice existed for childless couples or for those whose children had already grown up. Luchesio and Buonadonna wanted another alternative, a way of sharing in religious life, but outside the cloister.

To meet this desire, Francis set up the Secular Franciscan Order. Francis wrote a simple Rule for the Third Order (Secular Franciscans) at first; Pope Honorius III approved a more formally worded Rule in 1221.

The charity of Luchesio drew the poor to him, and, like many other saints, he and Buonadonna seemed never to lack the resources to help these people.

One day Luchesio was carrying a crippled man he had found on the road. A frivolous young man came up and asked, "What poor devil is that you are carrying there on your back?" "I am carrying my Lord Jesus Christ," responded Luchesio. The young man immediately begged Luchesio's pardon.

Luchesio and Buonadonna both died on April 28, 1260. He was beatified in 1273. Local tradition referred to Buonadonna as "blessed" though the title was not given officially.

Quote: Francis used to say, "Whoever curses a poor man does an injury to Christ, whose noble image he wears, the image of him who made himself poor for us in this world" (1 Celano, #76).

Comment: It is easy to mock the poor, to trample on their God-given dignity. Mother Teresa of Calcutta often referred to poverty as Christ's "distressing disguise." Since it is so easy to make people feel unwanted — the poor, the sick, the mentally or physically handicapped, the aged, the unemployed — resisting that temptation indicates the level of generosity in our lives. If the followers of Francis see Christ in the poor as Luchesio and Buonadonna did, they enrich the Church and keep it faithful to its Lord.

Saint Joseph Benedict Cottolengo (III)
1786-1842

In some ways Joseph exemplified Saint Francis' advice, "Let us begin to serve the Lord God, for up to now we have made little or no progress" (*1 Celano*, #103).

Joseph was the eldest of twelve children. Born in Piedmont, he was ordained for the Diocese of Turin in 1811. Frail health and difficulty in school were obstacles he overcame to reach ordination.

During Joseph's lifetime Italy was torn by civil war while the poor and the sick suffered from neglect. Inspired by reading the life of Saint Vincent de Paul and moved by the human suffering all around him, Joseph rented some rooms to nurse the sick of his parish and recruited local young women to staff it.

In 1832 at Voldocco, Joseph founded the House of Providence which served many different groups (the sick, the elderly, students, the mentally ill, the blind). All of this was financed by contributions. Popularly called "the University of Charity," this testimonial to God's goodness was serving eight thousand people by the time of Joseph's beatification in 1917.

To carry on his work, Joseph organized two religious communities, the Brothers of Saint Vincent de Paul and the Sisters of Saint Vincent de Paul. Joseph, who had joined the Secular Franciscans as a young man, was canonized in 1934.

Quote: "Almighty, eternal, just and merciful God, grant us in our misery [the grace] to do for You alone what we know You want us to do, and always to desire what pleases You. Thus, inwardly cleansed, interiorly enlightened, and inflamed by the fire of the Holy Spirit, may we be able to follow in the footprints of Your beloved Son, our Lord Jesus Christ. And by Your grace alone, may we make our way to You, Most High, Who live and rule in perfect Trinity and simple Unity, and are glorified, God all-powerful forever and ever. Amen" (Saint Francis, *Letter to the Entire Order*).

Comment: How do we know God's will for us? Is that will static? Joseph did not begin the work for which he is most famous until twenty-one years after his ordination. Years of praying and searching certainly kept Joseph alert to God's call. However well we have responded to our neighbor's need in the past, God is surely calling us to greater generosity. That must have been what Francis meant when he said, "Let us begin to serve the Lord God."

Blessed Thomas Bullaker, Henry Heath, John Woodcock, Arthur Bell and Charles Meehan (I)
d. 1642-1679

In 1987, sixty-three priests and twenty-two lay people martyred in England, Scotland or Wales between 1584 and 1689 were beatified. These five friars were part of that group.

Thomas Bullaker (1602-42) was born in England, studied for the priesthood in Spain, joined the Order there and served in Avila and Segovia before his twelve-year ministry in England. He was hanged, drawn and quartered at Tyburn.

Henry Heath (1603-43) studied at Cambridge and became a Catholic at age twenty-four. He joined the friars and studied for the priesthood in Douai, Belgium. Henry was captured immediately upon returning to England and was martyred at Tyburn.

Arthur Bell (1591-1643) was born to a wealthy family and studied in Belgium and Spain where he was ordained in 1618. He worked in England for about nine years before his capture, condemnation and then execution at Tyburn.

John Woodcock (1603-46) joined the friars in Belgium and was ordained there in 1634. He knew Heath and Bell.

Charles Meehan (1640-79) belonged to the Irish province. On his return to Ireland after finishing his studies in Rome, he was shipwrecked off the coast of Wales in 1678. He was martyred the following year.

Quote: During the homily at the beatification Mass, Pope John Paul II said: "The martyrs whose glory the Church proclaims today gave their lives in order to bear witness to the Truth. They suffered death. By suffering death, they professed their faith in Life, in that Life which was revealed to the world in the Resurrection of Christ" (1987 LOR 48:6).

Comment: During the homily cited above, the pope added, "We must all rejoice that the hostilities between Christians, which so shaped the age of these martyrs, are over, replaced by fraternal love and mutual esteem." The pope praised the progress "towards fuller communion between Anglicans and Catholics."

Blessed Ceferino Giménez Malla (III)
1861-1936

The first Gypsy to be beatified was a martyr and a Secular Franciscan. Ceferino was born in Fraga (Spain). He had a successful business, buying and selling horses. Ceferino and his wife had no children though they adopted one of his wife's nieces. He attended Mass frequently and joined the Secular Franciscan Order. Always generous to the poor, he was known as a reconciler among Gypsies.

During the Spanish Civil War, he was arrested for defending a priest who had been dragged through the streets of Barbastro and for having a rosary. As the firing squad prepared to kill him, Ceferino clutched his rosary and cried out *"Viva Cristo Rey!"* (Long live Christ the King!) He was beatified in 1997.

Quote: At Ceferino's beatification, Pope John Paul II said: "His life shows how Christ is present in the various peoples and races, and that all are called to holiness which is attained by keeping his commandments and remaining in his love (John 15:11)" (1997 LOR, 19:6).

Comment: Ceferino shows us that Christ's love is not limited by race or culture. The daily living out of his baptism prepared Ceferino for making the supreme sacrifice of his life. For better or for worse, the decisions we make today prepare us for future decisions.

Mother Ignatius Hayes (III)
1823-1894

Some people have been intrigued since childhood by Saint Francis and his followers. Others were adults when they first contacted the Franciscan movement; such was the case with Mother Ignatius Hayes.

Elizabeth was the eighth child of an Anglican clergyman in England. As a young woman she joined the Butler Anglican sisterhood, which devoted itself to educational reform. Prompted by the Oxford Movement, Elizabeth joined the Church of Rome. At the direction of Dr. Manning (later Archbishop of Westminster), she entered a community dedicated to caring for the poor and the sick. Later she became a Third Order sister in Scotland.

Desiring to found a congregation of her own, Elizabeth (now Sister Mary Ignatius) obtained permission to come to the United States. After a short stay in Boston, she went to St. Paul, Minnesota, where Bishop Grace sent her to the Indian reservation at Belle Prairie, Minnesota. There she worked with the children of poor Canadian settlers.

In 1872 she began the first Franciscan convent in Minnesota. Her sisters established a girls' boarding school. Another foundation in Augusta, Georgia, followed.

In 1880 Mother Ignatius went to Rome where, at the suggestion of Pope Leo XIII, she established a community of her sisters. The following year she moved the motherhouse of her community from Minnesota to Rome. Eventually her community would become three groups: Missionary Sisters of the Immaculate Conception (Rome), Franciscan Sisters of the Immaculate Conception (Little Falls, Minnesota) and Franciscan Sisters of the Immaculate Conception of Rock Island, Illinois.

In 1893 Mother Ignatius wanted to visit her sisters in America. Becoming sick in Naples, she was forced to return to Rome where she died on May 6, 1894.

Quote: In her diary Mother Ignatius wrote: "The lives of the saints depress me, bringing back the longing for a life of penance — for labor among the sick and poor...seemed all their life. In hours of desolation it seems as if I had not grace nor strength enough. The greatest miracle is myself, that I should be a Catholic, a religious, a Franciscan. Yet, I am so weak bodily, so sensitive mentally, that left to myself a moment I should not bear up against the least cross."

Comment: The lives of the saints can sap our courage if we forget that God's grace is the root of all holiness. Although reading the lives of the saints sometimes depressed Mother Ignatius, she was also encouraged by the courage and self-sacrifice of other followers of Jesus. As Saint Paul learned, in human weakness God's power reaches perfection (see 2 Corinthians 12:9).

Saint Catharine of Bologna (II)
1413-1463

Some Franciscan saints led fairly public lives; Catharine represents the saints who served the Lord in obscurity.

Catharine, born in Bologna, was related to the nobility in Ferrara and was educated at court there. She received a liberal education at the court and developed some interest and talent in painting. In later years as a Poor Clare, Catharine sometimes did manuscript illumination and also painted miniatures.

At the age of seventeen, she joined a group of religious women in Ferrara. Four years later the whole group joined the Poor Clares in that city. Jobs as convent baker and portress preceded her selection as novice mistress.

In 1456 she and fifteen other sisters were sent to establish a Poor Clare monastery in Florence. As abbess Catharine worked to preserve the peace of the new community. Her reputation for holiness drew many young women to the Poor Clare life. She was canonized in 1712.

Quote: Catharine wrote a book on the seven spiritual weapons to be used against temptation. "Jesus Christ gave up his life that we might live," she said. "Therefore, whoever wishes to carry the cross for his sake must take up the proper weapons for the contest, especially those mentioned here. First, diligence; second, distrust of self; third, confidence in God; fourth, remembrance of the Passion; fifth, mindfulness of one's own death; sixth, remembrance of God's glory; seventh, the injunctions of Sacred Scripture following the example of Jesus Christ in the desert" (*On the Seven Spiritual Weapons*).

Comment: Appreciating Catharine's life in a Poor Clare monastery may be hard for us. "It seems like such a waste," we may be tempted to say. Through prayer, penance and charity to her sisters, Catharine drew close to God. Our goal is the same as hers even if our paths are different.

Saint Ivo of Brittany (III)
1253-1303

We don't often associate Franciscan saints with judges, but Ivo, nick-named "advocate of the poor," was both.

Ivo was born of noble parents in northern France. Early in life he told himself, "I must become a saint." He always kept that goal in mind. Ivo studied theology and law (canon and civil) at the Universities of Paris and Orleans. In both schools he fasted and attended daily Mass, visiting the sick regularly.

Ivo was ordained for the Diocese of Trequier and joined the Secular Franciscans after his ordination. Appointed a judge in the Church courts — first in Rennes and later in Trequier — Ivo placed his parish in the care of an administrator. Ivo developed a reputation for being a fair judge and for helping the poor, the widows and the orphans obtain a fair hearing. His personal life was ascetic: fasting, hair shirt, coarse food.

Eventually Ivo resigned his judgeship to care personally for his parish. His sermons, like those of Francis, were clear and simple. The poor found him a generous source of alms and of spiritual advice. Ivo was canonized in 1347.

Quote: "We must be prepared to take on new functions and new duties in every sector of human activity and especially in the sector of world society, if justice is really to be put into practice.... We should not forget the growing number of persons who are often abandoned by their families and by the community: the old, orphans, the sick and all kinds of people who are rejected" (1971 Synod of Bishops, *Justice in the World*, #1).

Comment: Giving preference to the most aggressive people or to the richest people is easy enough to do. G.K. Chesterton has written: "The rules of a club are occasionally in favor of the poor members. The drift of a club is always in favor of the rich ones" (*Orthodoxy*, page 41). Trying to be even-handed with everyone is not always easy and the job is never completely finished. Justice concerns all of us — not simply the lawyers and the judges.

Saint Ignatius of Laconi (I)
1701-1781

Ignatius is another sainted begging brother.

He was the second of seven children of peasant parents in Sardinia. His path to the Franciscans was unusual. During a serious illness, Ignatius vowed to become a Capuchin if he recovered. He regained his health but ignored the promise. A riding accident prompted him to renew the pledge, which he acted on the second time; he was twenty then. Ignatius's reputation for self-denial and charity led to his appointment as the official beggar for the friars in Cagliari. He fulfilled that task for forty years; he was blind the last two years.

While on his rounds, Ignatius would instruct the children, visit the sick and urge sinners to repent. The people of Cagliari were inspired by his kindness and his faithfulness to his work. He was canonized in 1951.

Quote: "And I used to work with my hands, and I [still] desire to work; and I firmly wish that all my brothers give themselves to honest work. Let those who do not know how [to work] learn, not from desire of receiving wages for their work but as an example and in order to avoid idleness. And when we are not paid for our work, let us have recourse to the table of the Lord, seeking alms from door to door" (Saint Francis, *Testament*).

Comment: Why did the people of Cagliari support the friars? These followers of Francis worked hard but rarely at jobs that paid enough to live on. Under these conditions Saint Francis allowed them to beg. The life of Ignatius reminds us that everything God considers worthwhile does not have a high-paying salary attached to it.

Mother Teresa O'Neil (III)
1843-1926

Positions of great responsibility in God's Church are often filled by men and women who radiate the love of Christ and who can inspire others to do likewise. Such a woman was Mother Teresa.

Mary Anne O'Neil, daughter of John and Bridget Williams O'Neil, was born in New York City. Her family later moved to Fort Lee, New Jersey, where Father Pamfilo da Magliano (November 16) visited in 1859. At that time he invited her to join the newly established congregation of Franciscan sisters in Allegany, New York.

Mary Anne's parents were opposed to her decision at first, but finally relented. She was invested on December 8, 1859, and took the name Mary Teresa. For several years she furthered her education and collected funds for a girls' academy that had opened in Allegany in 1860. A two-story brick building was completed in 1861 and was named St. Elizabeth's Convent and Academy in honor of Saint Elizabeth of Hungary (November 17).

The Civil War made life difficult in the new academy, but the generosity of the townspeople and nearby farmers enabled the sisters to keep the academy and convent running. In 1863 Sister Mary Teresa was certified as a public school teacher and for a short time taught in the publicly financed school in Allegany. In 1864 Father Pamfilo appointed her superior of the community; she held that position for fifty-five years (two by appointment and fifty-three by election).

At St. Elizabeth Academy in Allegany and at St. Anthony School in lower Manhattan, she served as teacher and principal. During her years as General Superior, the Allegany sisters expanded their educational apostolate and also began hospitals and homes for young working men and women. In 1878 the congregation initiated work in Jamaica, West Indies. Soon a group of sisters already established there was incorporated into the Allegany community. By 1926 the Jamaican sisters had opened two secondary schools, nine elementary schools and a teachers' training college. Mother Teresa died on May 12, 1926.

Quote: Sister Veronica Rodrigues, archivist of the Allegany sisters, writes: "Mother Teresa has been described as a 'valiant woman,' an 'ascetic religious,' an 'excellent administrator,' a 'kindly Sister,' a 'charitable person,' etc. She was greatly respected by the students of the schools in which she taught and loved for her concern about their welfare. The townspeople of Allegany paid tribute to her on various occasions — her jubilee celebrations and at her death. Her sisters showed their confidence and love of her by reelecting her to the highest office in the Congregation. Her life was one of trials...but she weathered all trusting in God and his Mother to help her solve her problems."

Comment: Mother Teresa was concerned that her sisters show the fraternal charity so prized by Saint Francis. The trials and obstacles she faced in furthering the work of her community no doubt led her to identify with Saint Paul. Mother Teresa often quoted the advice on love he wrote to the Corinthians (see 1 Corinthians 13). She knew as Paul did that all her gifts for administration and leadership still were secondary to charity.

May 16

Saint Margaret of Cortona (III)
1247-1297

Some people have called Margaret the Mary Magdalene of the Franciscan movement.

Margaret was born of farming parents in Laviano, Tuscany. Her mother died when Margaret was seven; life with her stepmother was so difficult that Margaret moved out. For nine years she lived with Arsenio, though they were not married, and she bore him a son. In those years, she had doubts about her situation. Somewhat like Saint Augustine she prayed for purity — but not just yet.

One day she was waiting for Arsenio and was instead met by his dog. The animal led Margaret into the forest where she found Arsenio murdered. This crime shocked Margaret into a life of penance. She and her son returned to Laviano where she was not well received by her stepmother. They then went to Cortona, where her son eventually became a friar.

In 1277, three years after her conversion, Margaret became a Franciscan tertiary. Under the direction of her confessor, who sometimes had to order her to moderate her self-denial, she pursued a life of prayer and penance at Cortona. There she established a hospital and founded a congregation of tertiary sisters. The poor and humble Margaret was, like Francis, devoted to the Eucharist and to the passion of Jesus. These devotions fueled her great charity and drew sinners to her for advice and inspiration. She was canonized in 1728.

Quote: "Let us raise ourselves from our fall and not give up hope as long as we free ourselves from sin. Jesus Christ came into this world to save sinners. 'O come, let us worship and bow down, let us kneel before the LORD, our

Maker!' (Psalm 95:6). The Word calls us to repentance, crying out: 'Come to me, all you that are weary and are carrying heavy burdens and I will give you rest' (Matthew 11:28). There is, then, a way to salvation if we are willing to follow it" (*Letter of Saint Basil the Great*).

Comment: Seeking forgiveness is sometimes difficult work. It is made easier by meeting people who, without trivializing our sins, assure us that God rejoices over our repentance. Being forgiven lifts a weight and prompts us to acts of charity.

May 17

Saint Paschal Baylon (I)
1540-1592

In Paschal's lifetime the Spanish empire in the New World was at the height of its power, though France and England were soon to reduce its influence. The sixteenth century has been called the Golden Age of the Church in Spain, for it gave birth to Ignatius of Loyola, Francis Xavier, Teresa of Avila, John of the Cross, Peter of Alcantara (October 22), Francis Solano (July 14) and Salvator of Horta (March 18).

Paschal's Spanish parents were poor but pious. Between the ages of seven and twenty-four he worked as a shepherd and began a life of mortification. He was able to pray on the job and was especially attentive to the church bell which rang at the Elevation during Mass. Paschal had a very honest streak in him. He once offered to pay owners of crops for any damage his animals caused!

In 1564 Paschal joined the Friars Minor and gave himself wholeheartedly to a life of penance. Though he was urged to study for the priesthood, he chose to be a brother. At various times he served as porter, cook, gardener and official beggar.

Paschal was careful to observe the vow of poverty. He would never waste any food or anything given for the use of the friars. When he was porter and took care of the poor coming to the door, he developed a reputation for great generosity. The friars sometimes tried to moderate his liberality!

Paschal spent his spare moments praying before the Blessed Sacrament. In time many people sought his wise counsel.

People flocked to his tomb immediately after his burial; miracles were reported promptly. In 1690 Paschal was canonized; in 1897 he was named patron of eucharistic congresses and societies.

Quote: "Meditate well on this: Seek God above all things. It is right for you to seek God before and above everything else, because the majesty of God wishes you to receive what you ask for. This will also make you more ready to serve God and will enable you to love him more perfectly" (Saint Paschal).

Comment: Prayer before the Blessed Sacrament occupied much of Saint Francis' energy. Most of his letters were to promote devotion to the Eucharist. Paschal shared that concern.

An hour in prayer before our Lord in the Eucharist could teach all of us a great deal. Some holy and busy Catholics today find that their work is enriched by those minutes regularly spent in prayer and meditation.

May 18

Saint Felix of Cantalice (I)
1515-1587

Felix was the first Capuchin ever canonized. In fact, when he was born, the Capuchins did not yet exist as a distinct group within the Franciscans.

Born of humble but God-fearing parents in the Rieti Valley, Felix worked as a farmhand and a shepherd until he was twenty-eight. He developed the habit of praying while he worked.

In 1543 he joined the Capuchins. When the guardian explained the hardships of that way of life, Felix answered: "Father, the austerity of your Order does not frighten me. I hope, with God's help, to overcome all the difficulties which will arise from my own weakness."

Three years later Felix was assigned to the friary in Rome as its official beggar. Because he was a model of simplicity and charity, he edified many people during the forty-two years he performed that service for his confreres.

As he made his rounds, he worked to convert hardened sinners and to feed the poor as did his good friend, St. Philip Neri, who founded the Oratory, a community of priests serving the poor of Rome. When Felix wasn't talking on his rounds, he was praying the rosary. The people named him "Brother Deo Gratias" (thanks be to God) because he was always using that blessing.

When Felix was an old man, his superior had to order him to wear sandals to protect his health. Around the same time a certain cardinal offered to suggest to Felix's superiors that he be freed of begging so that he could devote more time to prayer. Felix talked the cardinal out of that idea. Felix was canonized in 1712.

Quote: "And let us refer all good to the most high and supreme lord God, and acknowledge that every good is His, and thank Him for everything, [He] from Whom all good things come. And may He, the Highest and Supreme, Who alone is true God, have and be given and receive every honor and reverence, every praise and blessing, every thanks and glory, for every good is His, He Who alone is good. And when we see or hear an evil [person] speak or act or blaspheme God, let us speak well and act well and praise God (cf. Rm 12:21), Who is blessed forever (Rm 1:25)" (Saint Francis, *Rule of 1221*, Chapter 17).

Comment: Grateful people make good beggars. Francis told his friars that if they gave the world good example, the world would support them. Felix's life proves the truth of that advice. In referring all blessings back to their source (God), Felix encouraged people to works of charity for the friars and for others.

Saint Theophilus of Corte (I)
1676-1740

If we expect saints to do marvelous things continually and to leave us many memorable quotes, we are bound to be disappointed with Saint Theophilus. The mystery of God's grace in a person's life, however, has a beauty all its own.

Theophilus was born in Corsica of rich and noble parents. As a young man he entered the Friars Minor and soon showed his love for solitude and prayer. After admirably completing his studies, he was ordained and assigned to a *ritiro* (house of recollection) near Subiaco. Inspired by the austere life of the friars there, he founded other such houses in Corsica and Tuscany.

Though he was always somewhat sickly, Theophilus generously served the needs of God's people in the confessional, in the sickroom and at the graveside. Worn out by his labors, he died on June 17, 1740. He was canonized in 1930.

Quote: Francis used to say, "Let us begin, brothers, to serve the Lord God, for up to now we have made little or no progress" (*1 Celano*, #103).

Comment: There is a certain dynamism in all the saints that prompts them to find ever more selfless ways of responding to God's grace. As time went on, Theophilus gave more and more singlehearted service to God and to God's sons and daughters.

Honoring the saints will make no sense unless we are thus drawn to live as generously as they did. Their holiness can never substitute for our own.

May 20

Saint Bernardine of Siena (I)
1380-1444

According to Pope Pius II, Bernardine was "a second Paul." Bernardine came from a knightly family in Siena. His parents died before he was seven. After studying theology and canon law in Siena, he joined the Franciscans in 1402. He entered the group known as the Observants, the forerunners of today's Friars Minor, and was eventually known, with John of Capistrano (October 23), James of the Marche (November 28) and Albert of Sarteano, as one of the "four pillars of the Observance."

Bernardine was the greatest preacher of his day; sometimes 30,000 people came to hear him. In his time many Italian city-states were torn by rival factions, each with its own party emblem. Looking for a way of inviting them to move beyond these factions, Bernardine preached on the Holy Name of Jesus, the name before which

> every knee should bend,
> in heaven and on earth and
> under the earth

and every tongue should confess
    that Jesus Christ is Lord,
    to the glory of God the Father (Philippians 2:10-11).

Bernardine had banners made with the emblem YHS (abbreviation of the Greek word for Jesus). He organized processions behind these to symbolize the surpassing of old allegiances. Some complained that this was superstitious and had Bernardine brought before Church authorities to explain himself; he was vindicated.

In 1418 the Duke of Milan was so impressed with Bernardine's Lenten sermons that he sent a messenger with some money for the friar. Bernardine refused to accept it, but led the messenger to the local prison and had him pay the debts of several people there.

Bernardine frequently preached against luxury and extravagance. Several times his sermons concluded with a bonfire, "the Devil's Castle," into which people were invited to throw dice, playing cards, wigs, perfume, high-heeled shoes and so on. Bernardine also vigorously denounced usury, the charging of excessive interest on loans.

Bernardine encouraged learning among the Franciscans as a preparation for preaching; he worked tirelessly for reform among the friars.

Bernardine three times declined the offer to be made a bishop. He was canonized six years after his death.

Quote: "The name of Jesus is the glory of preachers, because the shining splendor of that name causes his word to be proclaimed and heard. And how do you think such an immense, sudden and dazzling light of faith came into the world, if not because Jesus was preached? Was it not through the brilliance and sweet savor of this name that 'God called us into his marvelous light' (1 Peter 2:9)?" (Saint Bernardine, *Sermon* #49)

Comment: By promoting devotion to the Holy Name, Bernardine hoped to draw many Italians out of the political factionalism which was destroying their cities. He also hoped they would live up to the name by which they were saved and would, in the words of Saint Paul, lead a life worthy of their calling (Ephesians 4:1). The question of allegiances is an open one until each person's death.

Saint Crispin of Viterbo (I)
1668-1750

Crispin, who lived during the Age of Enlightenment, showed the enlightenment that gospel living provides.

Born in Orvieto, Peter was apprenticed to a shoemaker. In 1693 he received the Capuchin habit and the name Crispin. After serving as a cook at Tolfa and Albano, he was the official beggar of the friary in Orvieto for almost forty years.

He developed a reputation for curing the sick and catechized those he encountered in his work. The poor and needy recognized him as their friend. One of Crispin's favorite sayings was, "God's power creates us, his wisdom governs us, his mercy saves us." He was canonized in 1982.

Quote: During his homily at Crispin's canonization, Pope John Paul II said that the human family is frequently "tempted by false autonomy, by denial of Gospel values, for which it necessarily needs saints, that is, models who concretely express by their lives the reality of Transcendence, the values of the Revelation and Redemption achieved by Christ" (1982 LOR 26:1).

Comment: Henri de Lubac, S.J., once wrote, "We should have a great love for our age, but make no concessions to the spirit of the age, so that in us the Christian mystery may never lose its sap" (*The Splendor of the Church*, page 183). Crispin appreciated the people whom God brought into his life and the historical period in which God placed him. Crispin became a living gospel for his confreres and for the people of Orvieto. His holiness encouraged them to live out their baptism more generously.

Saint Mary Ann of Jesus of Paredes (III)
1614-1645

Mary Ann grew close to God and his people during her short life. The youngest of eight, Mary Ann was born in Quito, Ecuador, which had been brought under Spanish control in 1534. She joined the Secular Franciscans and led a life of prayer and penance at home, leaving her parents' house only to go to church and to perform some work of charity. She established in Quito a clinic and a school for Africans and indigenous Americans. When a plague broke out, she nursed the sick and died shortly thereafter.

She was canonized by Pope Pius XII in 1950.

Quote: "At times when especially impelled by love for God and fellowmen, she afflicted herself severely to expiate the sins of others. Oblivious then to the world around her and wrapped in ecstasy, she had a foretaste of eternal happiness. Thus transformed and enriched by God's grace she was filled with zeal to care not only for her own salvation, but also for that of others to the utmost of her ability. She generously relieved the miseries of the poor and soothed the pains of the sick. And when severe public disasters such as earthquakes and plagues terrified and afflicted her fellow citizens, she strove by prayer, expiation, and the offering of her own life to obtain from the Father of mercies what she could not accomplish by human effort" (Pius XII).

Comment: Francis of Assisi overcame himself (and his upbringing) when he kissed the man afflicted with leprosy. If our self-denial does not lead to charity, the penance is being practiced for the wrong reason. The penances of Mary Ann made her more sensitive to the needs of others and more courageous in trying to serve those needs.

June 1

John Patrick Doyle (III)
1874-1952

The history and growth of the Third Order Regular of Saint Francis in the United States is closely connected with the life and work of this zealous Franciscan priest.

Born near Thules, County Tipperary, Ireland, John Patrick migrated with his parents to the United States in 1881; they settled in Brooklyn, New York. After graduating in 1897 from St. Francis College (Brooklyn), John decided to become a diocesan priest. He received his doctorate in theology in Rome and was ordained in 1901.

After several years as an assistant pastor in the Brooklyn diocese, Father Doyle was appointed professor of philosophy at St. Francis College and chaplain to the Franciscan Brothers of Brooklyn who ran the college. Two years later he became an assistant pastor again. In 1910, with his bishop's permission, Father Doyle entered the Third Order Regular at Loretto, Pennsylvania.

He soon became president of St. Francis College in Loretto, Pennsylvania, where he reorganized the curriculum. In 1912 Father Doyle began St. Francis Seminary there for the education of diocesan and Third Order Regular priests. All the students were inspired by the holiness of his life. He was fondly known by the clergy and members of his Order as "Doctor Doyle." The friars benefited from his service as minister provincial (1924-37 and 1947-48).

When Father Doyle died on June 2, 1952, hundreds of priests — many coming from distant places — attended his funeral.

Quote: Father Doyle liked to quote the Italian proverb *"Corragio, il diavolo è morto"* ("Have courage, the devil is dead"). Another favorite expression was "You would be surprised at what you could do if you tried."

Comment: Like Jesus on that first Easter night, effective leaders in Christ's Church often call Christians to have courage, not to adopt the fear that the devil always encourages. Throughout his life Father Doyle followed Saint Paul's command to "encourage the fainthearted, help the weak, be patient with all of them" (1 Thessalonians 5:14). We can almost always live out the gospel with greater courage than we have shown before.

June 2

Christopher Bernsmeyer (I)
1777-1858

An interest in caring for pilgrims led Father Bernsmeyer to see an even greater need and to establish a community of sisters who would aid the Church's healing ministry. The results can still be seen in Europe and the United States.

Christopher Bernsmeyer was born at Werl in eastern Westphalia, Germany. When he was twenty-four he entered the Franciscan province of the Holy Cross. After finishing his theological studies in Münster, he was ordained in 1805. Soon afterward he became interested in caring for the pilgrims to the Marian shrine at Telgte near Münster.

When the Franciscan house in Münster was closed by Napoleon in 1812, Father Bernsmeyer moved to Telgte, where he assisted the parish priest in caring for the pilgrims. His habits of self-denial enabled him to help the poor. Seeing a need to provide care for the sick in their own homes, he established a congregation of sisters for that purpose. In 1848 these Sisters of Charity of Saint Francis opened St. Roch's Hospital in Telgte. They continued their home nursing apostolate.

In 1847 their Rule and statutes were approved by Father Alardus Bartscher, the nearby Franciscan minister provincial. When the new community began to suffer from defections and dissensions, the Bishop of Münster took over direction of the congregation and made Father Bernsmeyer an honorary chairman. The community became a Franciscan congregation in 1902 and took the name Hospital Sisters of the Third Order of Saint Francis.

On June 2, 1858, Father Christopher Bernsmeyer died; he is buried in the sisters' cemetery at St. Roch's Hospital (Telgte).

In 1875 Sister Angelica Ratte of this community led twenty sisters to the United States. Bishop Peter Baltes of Alton, Illinois, had invited them to establish hospitals and home nursing programs in his diocese. A province of this congregation is headquartered in Springfield, Illinois.

Quote: In 1855 when Father Bernsmeyer celebrated the fiftieth anniversary of his ordination, a Münster newspaper said: "On this occasion it was evident how much the jubilarian had grown in the love and esteem of all through his indefatigable activity in the confessional and in the care of the sick, as well as by his friendly and lovable personality during more than forty years in our district."

Comment: Like Saint Francis, Father Bernsmeyer attracted people to the gospel life he followed. Humility, patience and unwavering trust in divine providence were his characteristic virtues. His great devotion to the Blessed Mother inspired the people of Telgte and sustained him through the trials and difficulties of beginning a religious community and then seeing its direction pass to others.

Joseph Perez (I)
1890-1928

"**T**he blood of martyrs is the seed of the Church," said Tertullian in the third century. Joseph Perez carried on that tradition.

Joseph was born in Coroneo, Mexico, and joined the Franciscans when he was seventeen. Because of Mexico's civil unrest at that time (the forces of Pancho Villa had crossed into New Mexico on a raid the previous year), he was forced to take his philosophy and theology studies in California.

After ordination at Mission Santa Barbara, he returned to Mexico and served at Jerecuaro from 1922 on. The persecution under the presidency of Plutarco Calles (1924-28) forced Joseph to wear various disguises as he traveled around to visit the Catholics. In 1927 Church property was nationalized, Catholic schools were closed, and foreign priests and nuns were deported.

One day Joseph and several others were captured while returning from a secretly-held Mass. Father Perez was stabbed to death by soldiers a few miles from Celaya on June 2, 1928.

When Joseph's body was later brought in procession to Salvatierra, it was buried there amid cries of *"Viva, Cristo Rey!"* (Long live Christ the King!).

Quote: Father Joseph's memorial card includes these words: "May almighty God grant that our prayer, which is supported by the bloody sacrifice of this martyr, may graciously appear in his sight and bring salvation to us and redemption to our country" (Marion A. Habig, O.F.M., *The Franciscan Book of Saints*, page 412).

Comment: The Catholic Church in Mexico today is much freer than it was in the 1920's. Catholicism is very much alive in Mexico today, nurtured in part by martyrs like Father Perez.

Saint Anthony of Padua (I)
1195-1231

Anthony was another would-be Franciscan missionary whom God called to other work.

His parents, Martin and Maria Bulhom, baptized him Fernando. In 1210 he joined the Canons of Saint Augustine in Lisbon. This monastery, however, was too close to Fernando's worldly friends and to the king's quarrels with the Church. Two years later Fernando was allowed to transfer to the monastery at Coimbra, a city a hundred miles north of Lisbon. There he studied Scripture and prepared for his ordination, which probably occurred in 1220.

After the bones of the first Franciscan martyrs in Morocco (January 16) were brought to Coimbra in 1220, Fernando told the friars begging at the monastery door, "Dearest brothers, gladly will I take the habit of your Order if you will promise that as soon as I do so you will send me to the land of the Saracens, there to reap the same reward as your holy martyrs and gain a share in their glory."

Since the friars' place in Coimbra was dedicated to Saint Anthony the Egyptian hermit, Fernando took that name. A year later he went to Morocco, but poor health forced him back.

His boat was sidetracked to Sicily where he joined the friars going to the 1221 Pentecost Chapter in Assisi. There Anthony saw Saint Francis and was assigned to the northern province where he served at the hermitage in Monte Paolo near Bologna.

In the summer of 1222 Anthony attended the ordination of several friars. At the dinner afterwards the superior asked one of the friars to preach. All the Dominicans and Franciscans present declined except Anthony. He amazed the friars with a marvelous sermon on Christ's obedience, even to death on a cross. A hidden talent was revealed!

Soon Anthony was appointed to teach theology to the friars in Bologna. His previous studies in Coimbra served him well at this time. Anthony the teacher always heeded the command Saint Francis addressed to him that this study of theology must not destroy the spirit of holy prayer and devotion. Indeed, Anthony's students learned Scripture from a man as holy as he was learned.

Anthony later received permission to preach throughout northern Italy, where heretics had recently won many followers. The Church's wealth was causing a bitter controversy, and the poor and simple lives of wandering dissident preachers contrasted sharply with the lives of many priests and bishops. Anthony won converts by his sermons and by his simple way of living.

In 1224 Anthony was sent to southern France, where the Albigensians had made many converts, to preach the gospel. There he earned the nickname "Hammer of Heretics." In fact, Anthony won over the dissidents as much by his holiness and great charity as by his learning.

In 1227 Anthony returned to northern Italy where he was made provincial of the friars in that area. He continued his popular preaching. Only in 1228 did Anthony come to Padua where he immediately won over the people. Thousands listened to his Lenten series in 1231. Under the influence of his preaching, the city of Padua later passed a law against the commonly accepted practice of imprisoning debtors until they paid off the complete debt.

In the spring of 1231 Anthony withdrew with his companions Brother Luke and Brother Roger to the friary at Camposampiero where he had a sort of treehouse built as a hermitage. There he prayed and prepared himself for death.

On June 13, 1231, he became very ill and asked to be taken back to Padua. At the friary in Arcella, on the way, Anthony received the last sacraments. Shortly before he died, he called out, "I see my Lord."

Anthony was canonized less than a year after his death and was named a Doctor of the Church in 1946.

Quote: "When a crystal is touched or struck by the rays of the sun, it gives forth brilliant sparks of light. When the man of faith is touched by the light of God's grace, he too must give forth sparks of light in his good words and deeds, and so bring God's light to others" (Saint Anthony, *Sermon* #274).

Comment: Anthony placed his preaching and writing talents at the service of the Church, with great results. Much of his success is attributable to the holiness of his life.

In our world of constant imitation, it is often difficult to find "the real thing." People who met Anthony of Padua knew they had seen and heard "the real thing."

Saint Albert Chmielowski (III)
1845-1916

Born in Igolomia near Kraków as the eldest of four children in a wealthy family, he was christened Adam. During the 1864 revolt against Czar Alexander III, Adam's wounds forced the amputation of his left leg.

His great talent for painting led to studies in Warsaw, Munich and Paris. Adam returned to Kraków and became a Secular Franciscan. In 1888 he took the name Albert when he founded the Brothers of the Third Order of Saint Francis, Servants to the Poor. They worked primarily with the homeless, depending completely on alms while serving the needy, regardless of age, religion or politics. A community of Albertine sisters was established later.

Pope John Paul II beatified him in 1983 and canonized him six years later.

Quote: The first reading at the canonization included Isaiah 58:6 ("Is not this the fast that I choose: to loose the bonds of injustice, to undo the thongs of the yoke, to let the oppressed go free, and to break every yoke?"). The pope referred to this passage and said: "This is the theology of messianic liberation, which contains what we are accustomed to calling today the 'option for the poor.'. . . In this tireless, heroic service on behalf of the marginalized and the poor, he [Albert] ultimately found his path. He found Christ. He took upon himself Christ's yoke and burden; he did not become merely 'one of those who give alms,' but became the brother to those he served. . . ." (1989 LOR 49:9).

Comment: Reflecting on his own priestly vocation, Pope John Paul II wrote in 1996 that Brother Albert had played a role in its formation "because I found in him a real spiritual support and example in leaving behind the world of art, literature and the theater, and in making the radical choice of a vocation to the priesthood" (*Gift and Mystery: On the Fiftieth Anniversay of My Priestly Ordination*, page 33). As a young priest, Karol Wotyla repaid his debt of gratitude by writing *The Brother of Our God*, a play about Brother Albert's life.

Venerable Matt Talbot (III)
1856-1925

Matt can be considered the patron of men and women struggling with alcoholism.

Matt was born in Dublin, where his father worked on the docks and had a difficult time supporting his family. After a few years of schooling, Matt obtained work as a messenger for some liquor merchants; there he began to drink excessively. For fifteen years — until he was thirty — Matt was an active alcoholic.

One day he decided to take "the pledge" for three months, make a general confession and begin to attend daily Mass. There is evidence that Matt's first seven years after taking the pledge were especially difficult. Avoiding his former drinking places was hard. He began to pray as intensely as he used to drink. He also tried to pay back people from whom he had borrowed or stolen money while he was drinking.

Most of his life Matt worked as a builder's laborer. He joined the Secular Franciscan Order and began a life of strict penance; he abstained from meat nine months a year. Matt spent hours every night avidly reading Scripture and the lives of the saints. He prayed the rosary conscientiously. Though his job did not make him rich, Matt contributed generously to the missions.

After 1923 his health failed and Matt was forced to quit work. He died on his way to church on Trinity Sunday. Fifty years later Pope Paul VI gave him the title venerable.

Quote: On an otherwise blank page in one of Matt's books, the following is written: "God console thee and make thee a saint. To arrive at the perfection of humility four things are necessary: to despise the world, to despise no one, to despise self, to despise being despised by others."

Comment: In looking at the life of Matt Talbot, we may easily focus on the later years when he had stopped drinking for some time and was leading a penitential life. Only alcoholic men and women who have stopped drinking can fully appreciate how difficult the earliest years of sobriety were for Matt.

He had to take one day at a time. So do the rest of us.

Saint Thomas More (III)
1477-1535

Thomas, who once wanted to be an obscure monk, found himself thrust into public attention by refusing to deny his conscience.

Thomas was born in Cheapside, London; his father was a knight, lawyer and eventually a judge. His mother died when Thomas was a child. After distinguished service as a page to Cardinal Morton, Archbishop of Canterbury and Chancellor of England, Thomas entered Oxford in 1492. An excellent student, he was also frugal and pious. Studies for the law followed in London.

Around 1498 Thomas considered entering the First Order of Saint Francis; it is believed that at this time he became a Secular Franciscan. In 1500-1504, he lived with the Carthusian monks in London but ultimately concluded God had not called him to that life. Daily Mass, fasting and wearing a hair shirt remained a part of his life.

Entering the king's service in 1518, More became Chancellor eleven years later. He tried to steer clear of Henry VIII's marriage case, but when Henry married Anne Boleyn and had Parliament declare him head of the Church in England, More resigned his office.

He was, however, too well known and respected throughout Europe for Henry to let him go quietly. Because Thomas would not swear to the Act of Supremacy, he was imprisoned in the Tower of London for fifteen months. Condemned on perjured evidence, More was beheaded on July 6, 1535.

Considered a patron of lawyers and university students, More was canonized in 1935.

Quote: As he was about to die, Thomas More told the crowd, "I die the king's good servant, but God's first."

Comment: Thomas More knew exactly how to keep himself alive, but he would not lie to do that, nor would he deny his conscience for Henry VIII. Priorities lead us into difficult decisions at times. Thomas More and Francis of Assisi differed in almost all the details of their lives, but they were very much alike in responding to God with all the courage and strength at their disposal.

Saint Joseph Cafasso (III)
1811-1860

Joseph is one of many saintly tertiary priests.

Even as a young man, Joseph loved to attend Mass and was known for his humility and fervor in prayer. After his ordination he was assigned to a seminary in Turin. There he worked especially against the spirit of Jansenism, an excessive preoccupation with sin and damnation. Joseph used the works of Saint Francis de Sales and Saint Alphonsus Ligouri to moderate the rigorism popular at the seminary.

Joseph recommended membership in the Secular Franciscan Order to priests. He urged devotion to the Blessed Sacrament and encouraged daily Communion. In addition to his teaching duties, Joseph was an excellent preacher, confessor and retreat master. Noted for his work with condemned prisoners, Joseph helped many of them die at peace with God.

Saint John Bosco was one of Joseph's pupils. Joseph urged John Bosco to establish the Salesians to work with the youth of Turin. Joseph was canonized in 1947.

Quote: "O admirable heights and sublime lowliness! O sublime humility! O humble sublimity! That the Lord of the universe, God and the Son of God, so humbles Himself that for our salvation He hides Himself under the little form of bread! Look, brothers, at the humility of God and pour out your hearts before Him! Humble yourselves, as well, that you may be exalted by Him. Therefore, hold back nothing of yourselves for yourselves so that He Who gives Himself totally to you may receive you totally" (Saint Francis, *Letter to the Entire Order*).

Comment: Devotion to the Eucharist gave energy to all Joseph's other activities. Long prayer before the Blessed Sacrament has been characteristic of many Catholics who have lived out the gospel well, Saint Francis, Bishop Sheen, Cardinal Bernadin and Mother Teresa among them.

Francisco de Porras (I)
d. 1633

When the Massachusetts Bay Colony was just beginning, Francisco was bringing Catholicism to the Hopi people in northern Arizona.

Although he was born in Spain, Francisco was ordained in Mexico in 1606. After serving as novice master for several years, he became a missionary in northern Arizona among the Hopis around 1621. In 1629 he and two companions came to the pueblo of Awatovi. After learning their language, Francisco preached to the Hopis and in four years baptized almost four thousand of them.

Medicine men jealous of Francisco's success tried several times to kill him. On June 28, 1633, they finally poisoned him.

The Peabody Museum of Harvard University made excavations at Awatovi between 1935 and 1939 and discovered the foundation of a church building believed to be that of Father Francisco. His work outlasted the 1680 Pueblo Revolt, for only after 1700 did a group of non-Christian Hopis destroy Awatovi.

Quote: "And all the brothers, wherever they may be, should remember that they gave themselves and abandoned their bodies to the Lord Jesus Christ. And for love of Him, they must make themselves vulnerable to their enemies, both visible and invisible, because the Lord says: Whoever loses his life for my sake will save it (cf. Lk 9:24) in eternal life (Mt 25:46)" (Saint Francis, *Rule of 1221*, Chapter 16).

Comment: Francisco de Porras certainly lived out these words of Saint Francis. The material and spiritual poverty of the friars should enable them to undertake dangerous work for the sake of God's kingdom. If Francisco had stayed home in the security of Spain, he might never have become an inspiration to later Franciscans.

Mother Mary Francis Bachman (III)
1824-1863

Mother Mary Francis responded to an urgent need in the Catholic Church in the United States and inspired many women to serve God as sisters.

Maria Anna Boll was born in Wenigumstadt, Bavaria. Working in her mother's store, Anna met Anthony Bachmann, a farmer whom she later married. In August of 1847, Anthony migrated to the United States; Anna and their son John Frederick arrived later that year. The Bolls joined them in the United States some time later.

In 1851 Anthony was fatally wounded at a construction site in Philadelphia. At his deathbed Anna promised to do the will of God as revealed to her in the future. Three months later her fourth child was born.

Barbara Boll, Anna's sister, had moved into the Bachmann home after Anthony's death. The two sisters and a friend began to think about starting a religious community. Anna consulted Father John Hespelein, C.SS.R., who wrote Bishop John Neumann (canonized 1977), then in Rome. After Pope Pius IX had advised Bishop Neumann to establish a congregation of Franciscan sisters in the United States rather than bring over some European sisters, the bishop received permission from the Franciscan minister general to invest the young women, receive their vows and instruct them in the Rule of Saint Francis.

The three women were invested in 1855 and made their final vows the following year. At first they took into the convent the sick, working girls, the aged and the orphaned. They also cared for the sick poor in their own homes. Teaching, missions in New York and a hospital in Philadelphia soon followed. Bishop James Wood, successor of Bishop Neumann, separated the New York sisters from the group in Philadelphia who remained under the leadership of Maria Anna Boll, now Mother Mary Francis. Mother Bernardine Dorn was appointed superior general for the sisters in Syracuse.

In 1861 Mother Francis sent sisters to Buffalo. On June 30, 1863, tuberculosis claimed her life. Later that year the Buffalo sisters formed a separate community under Mother Margaret (Barbara) Boll.

The two daughters of Mother Mary Francis eventually joined the Buffalo community. Her son John died at eighteen of typhus; Aloysius served as a diocesan priest in Buffalo for almost fifty years.

Quote: One of Mother Francis' characteristic sayings was "My confidence in Him is very great, and all my hopes are centered in Him in whose service we are engaged."

Comment: In her short life as a religious, Mother Francis lived what she taught: self-denial, fidelity to the vows and the Rule, concern for each sister, devotion to the Church and its Vicar. Her spiritual daughters — numbering at one time over four thousand in five communities — have imitated her holiness in all parts of the world.

June 30

Blessed Raymond Lull (III)
1235-1315

Raymond worked all his life to promote the missions and died a missionary to North Africa.

Raymond was born at Palma on the island of Mallorca in the Mediterranean Sea. He earned a position in the king's court there. One day a sermon inspired him to dedicate his life to working for the conversion of the Muslims in North Africa. He became a Secular Franciscan and founded a college where missionaries could learn the Arabic they would need in the missions. Retiring to solitude, he spent nine years as a hermit. During that time he wrote on all branches of knowledge, a work which earned him the title "Enlightened Doctor."

Raymond then made many trips through Europe to interest popes, kings and princes in establishing special colleges to prepare future missionaries. He achieved his goal in 1311 when the Council of Vienne ordered the creation of chairs of Hebrew, Arabic and Chaldean at the universities of Bologna, Oxford, Paris and Salamanca. At the age of seventy-nine, Raymond went to North Africa in 1314 to be a missionary himself. An angry crowd of Muslims stoned him in the city of Bougie. Genoese merchants took him back to Mallorca where he died. Raymond was beatified in 1514.

Quote: Thomas of Celano wrote of Saint Francis: "In vain does the wicked man persecute one striving after virtue, for the more he is buffeted, the more strongly will he triumph. As someone says, indignity strengthens a generous spirit" (*1 Celano*, #11)

Comment: Raymond worked most of his life to help spread the gospel. Indifference on the part of some Christian leaders and opposition in North Africa did not turn him from his goal.

Three hundred years later Raymond's work began to have an influence in the Americas. When the Spanish began to spread the gospel in the New World, they set up missionary colleges to aid the work. Blessed Junipero Serra (July 1) belonged to such a college.

July 1

Blessed Junipero Serra (I)
1713-1784

O nly one Franciscan is in the Hall of Fame in the Unites States Capitol, and that is Junipero Serra, representing the state of California!

Junipero was born in Petra on the island of Mallorca in the Mediterranean Sea. His parents, Antonio and Margarita, were farmers. Their son became a friar in 1729. Serra's friend and biographer Francisco Palou tells us that Junipero was then quite interested in the saints. "As a result of this devout exercise of reading the lives of the saints, there arose in him a warm desire from the time of his novitiate to imitate them insofar as it was possible. This type of reading caused in him the same effect as was produced in Saint Ignatius Loyola" (Maynard Geiger, O.F.M., *Palou's Life of Fray Junipero Serra*, page 4).

After his ordination in 1737, Junipero taught philosophy at the University of Palma. In 1750 he joined the missionary College of San Fernando and went to Mexico to work. After serving in the Sierra Gorde missions, he became novice master in Mexico City. In 1769 he was named president of the mission in Upper California (the Baja peninsula below the state of California).

Junipero soon traveled into the present-day United States. Over the years he founded nine of the twenty-one Franciscan missions that eventually stretched from San Diego to San Francisco: Mission San Diego and San Carlos Borromeo (1770), San Antonio and San Gabriel (1771), San Luis Obispo (1772), San Francisco and San Juan Capistrano (1776), Santa Clara (1777) and San Buenaventura (1782). Between 1770 and his death in 1784, Serra and his confreres baptized 5,808 Native Americans in what is now California.

73

In all these missions, Junipero and the friars introduced the Native Americans to more effective agricultural methods and showed them how to domesticate the animals needed for food and transportation. As the missions prospered, their fields and livestock attracted the envy of Spanish colonists and non-Christian Native Americans. Most of the missions were seized for personal gain after Mexico won its independence from Spain in 1821.

Junipero Serra died at Mission San Carlos on August 28, 1784, and is buried there. He was beatified in 1988.

Quote: On November 25, 1784, the superior of the College of San Fernando in Mexico City wrote about Junipero's death to the provincial of the friars in Mallorca: "He died like the just, in such circumstances that all those who were present shed tender tears and were of the opinion that his happy soul immediately went to heaven to enjoy the reward for his great and unbroken labors of thirty-four years, sustained for our beloved Jesus, whom he always had in his mind, suffering those inexplicable things for our redemption. So great was the charity he manifested...that it caused wonder not only in the minds of the ordinary people but also in persons of station, all proclaiming that the man was a saint and his actions those of an apostle" (Maynard Geiger, O.F.M., *The Life and Times of Junipero Serra, or The Man Who Never Turned Back*, vol. 2, page 392).

Comment: Junipero was physically small — only five feet, two inches — but very influential. He worked with all his strength to announce the reign of God. Surely his interest in the saints intensified his missionary ambitions. Holy men and women do make a difference in the lives of others.

July 4

Saint Elizabeth of Portugal (III)
1271-1336

E lizabeth's middle name could have been "peacemaker." She was related to another peacemaker, Elizabeth of Hungary (November 17).

Elizabeth lived in a violent age. The Portuguese had expelled the Muslims about a hundred years before her birth; the Spanish were fighting the Muslims up until 1492. And there was no shortage of wars among Christians.

Elizabeth's birth to Peter III of Aragon and Constance reconciled Peter to his father. As a young woman, the Portuguese Elizabeth was austere with herself but always generous with others. She married Denis, the king of Portugal. Shortly after the birth of their second child, Denis began living scandalously and was unfaithful to Elizabeth.

She continued her penances and her visits to the sick. She also made clothes for the poor and vestments for churches. The ever-compassionate Elizabeth established orphanages and arranged for poor girls to have the dowries they needed for marriage.

One day Elizabeth was washing the feet of a sick woman. The woman wouldn't let her wash one foot, which had a cancerous sore. Elizabeth did wash that foot and kissed the wound — which was immediately healed.

Elizabeth considered Denis' sins as more against God than against herself and prayed constantly for his conversion. Denis eventually came to his senses and begged his wife's forgiveness. At peace in her marriage, Elizabeth restored peace between Denis and his brother and ended a civil war between Denis and their son Alphonse.

After her husband's death in 1235, Elizabeth planned to enter the Poor Clares. Others, however, talked her into joining the Secular Franciscans so that she could continue her works of charity personally. She lived near the Poor Clares in Coimbra. After making a difficult journey to restore peace between her son and her grandson, she died. Elizabeth was canonized in 1625.

Quote: "The Lord granted me, Brother Francis, to begin to do penance in this way: While I was in sin, it seemed very bitter to me to see lepers. And the Lord Himself led me among them and I had mercy upon them. And when I left them that which seemed bitter to me was changed into sweetness of soul and body; and afterward I lingered a little and left the world" (Saint Francis, *Testament*).

Comment: The encounter of Francis with the man suffering from leprosy changed the Poverello's life forever. After that, works of charity which seemed nearly impossible became second nature to him. Elizabeth followed the same path of penance and great charity. Only the humble have any hope of becoming peacemakers like Elizabeth.

Blessed Gregory Grassi and Companions (I, III)
d. 1900

Christian missionaries have often gotten caught in the crossfire of wars against their own countries. When the governments of Britain, Germany, Russia and France forced substantial territorial concessions from the Chinese in 1898, anti-foreign sentiment grew very strong among many Chinese people.

Gregory Grassi was born in Italy in 1833, ordained in 1856 and sent to China five years later. Gregory was later ordained Bishop of North Shanxi. With fourteen other European missionaries and fourteen Chinese religious, he was martyred during the short but bloody Boxer Uprising of 1900.

Twenty-six of these martyrs were arrested on the orders of Yu Hsien, the governor of Shanxi province. They were hacked to death on July 9, 1900. Five of them were Friars Minor; seven were Franciscan Missionaries of Mary — the first martyrs of their congregation. Seven were Chinese seminarians and Secular Franciscans; four martyrs were Chinese laymen and Secular Franciscans. The other three Chinese laymen killed in Shanxi simply worked for the Franciscans and were rounded up with all the others. Three Italian Franciscans were martyred that same week in the province of Hunan. All these martyrs were beatified in 1946.

Quote: "Martyrdom is part of the Church's nature since it manifests Christian death in its pure form, as the death of unrestrained faith, which is otherwise hidden in the ambivalence of all human events. Through martyrdom the Church's holiness, instead of remaining purely subjective, achieves by God's grace the visible expression it needs. As early as the second century one who accepted death for the sake of Christian faith or Christian morals was looked on and revered as a *martus* (witness). The term is scriptural in that Jesus Christ is the 'faithful witness' absolutely (Rv 1:5; 3:14)" (Karl Rahner, *Theological Dictionary*, volume 2, pages 108-109).

Comment: Martyrdom is the occupational hazard of missionaries. Throughout China during the Boxer Uprising, 5 bishops, 50 priests, 2 brothers, 15 sisters and 40,000 Chinese Christians were killed. The 146,575 Catholics served by the Franciscans in China in 1906 had grown to 303,760 by 1924 and were served by 282 Franciscans and 174 local priests. Great sacrifices often bring great results.

Saint Nicholas Pick and Companions (I)
d. 1572

It is not always possible to choose when and how we will witness to our faith.

In 1568 the Low Countries revolted against Spain. In the northern part (now the Netherlands), the revolt was also directed against Catholicism. This rebellion ultimately led to the recognition in 1648 of an independent Republic of United Provinces (Netherlands).

Nicholas and his companions (eleven Franciscans and eight diocesan priests) are also known as "the martyrs of Gorcum," where they were arrested by Calvinist soldiers. They were taken to Briel and urged to renounce the Roman Catholic teaching on Christ's presence in the Eucharist and on the pope's primacy. They refused and were hung from crossbeams. The execution was clumsily handled; it took two hours for some of them to strangle. They were canonized in 1867.

Quote: " 'The hour is now at hand,' Father Nicholas said, 'to receive from the hand of the Lord the long desired reward of the struggle, the crown of eternal happiness.' He encouraged them not to fear death nor to lose through cowardice the crown prepared for them and soon to be placed on their brows. Finally he prayed that they would joyfully follow the path on which they saw him leading the way. With these and similar words he joyfully mounted the ladder without ceasing to exhort his companions until strangulation deprived him of the use of his voice" (from a contemporary account of the martyrdom).

Comment: Notice which teachings were presented to these martyrs. Turning the Eucharist into some vague remembrance of Christ and denying the leadership of the successor of Peter might have seemed easy. Nicholas and his companions knew these teachings were part of God's plan for his people, and so they would not deny their faith. Both the Eucharist and the successor of Peter will eventually be instrumental in restoring unity among Christians.

Saint Veronica Giuliani (II)
1660-1727

Veronica's desire to be like Christ crucified was answered with the stigmata.

Veronica was born in Mercatelli. It is said that when her mother Benedetta was dying she called her five daughters to her bedside and entrusted each of them to one of the five wounds of Jesus. Veronica was entrusted to the wound below Christ's heart.

At the age of seventeen, Veronica joined the Poor Clares directed by the Capuchins. Her father had wanted her to marry, but she convinced him to allow her to become a nun. In her first years in the monastery, she worked in the kitchen, infirmary, sacristy and served as portress. At the age of thirty-four, she was made novice mistress, a position she held for twenty-two years. When she was thirty-seven, Veronica received the stigmata. Life was not the same after that.

Church authorities in Rome wanted to test Veronica's authenticity and so conducted an investigation. She lost the office of novice mistress temporarily and was not allowed to attend Mass except on Sundays or holy days. Through all of this Veronica did not become bitter, and the investigation eventually restored her as novice mistress.

Though she protested against it, at the age of fifty-six she was elected abbess, an office she held for eleven years until her death. Veronica was very devoted to the Eucharist and to the Sacred Heart. She offered her sufferings for the missions. Veronica was canonized in 1839.

Quote: Thomas of Celano says of Francis: "All the pleasures of the world were a cross to him, because he carried the cross of Christ rooted in his heart. And therefore the stigmata shone forth exteriorly in his flesh, because interiorly that deeply set root was sprouting forth from his mind" (*2 Celano*, #211).

Comment: Why did God grant the stigmata to Francis and to Veronica? God alone knows the deepest reasons, but as Celano points out, the external sign of the cross is a confirmation of these saints' commitment to the cross in their lives. The stigmata that appeared in Veronica's flesh had taken root in her heart many years before. It was a fitting conclusion for her love of God and her charity toward her sisters.

Saint John Jones (I) and Saint John Wall (I)
c. 1530-1598; 1620-1679

These two friars were martyred in England in the sixteenth and seventeenth centuries for refusing to deny their faith.

John Jones was Welsh. He was ordained a diocesan priest and was twice imprisoned for administering the sacraments before leaving England in 1590. He joined the Franciscans at the age of sixty and returned to England three years later while Queen Elizabeth I was at the height of her power. John ministered to Catholics in the English countryside until his imprisonment in 1596. He was condemned to be hanged, drawn and quartered. John was executed on July 12, 1598.

John Wall was born in England but was educated at the English College of Douai, Belgium. Ordained in Rome in 1648, he entered the Franciscans in Douai several years later. In 1656 he returned to work secretly in England.

In 1678 Titus Oates worked many English people into a frenzy over an alleged papal plot to murder the king and restore Catholicism in that country. In that year Catholics were legally excluded from Parliament, a law which was not repealed until 1829. John Wall was arrested and imprisoned in 1678 and was executed the following year.

John Jones and John Wall were canonized in 1970.

Quote: "No one is a martyr for a conclusion; no one is a martyr for an opinion. It is faith that makes martyrs" (Cardinal Newman, *Discourses to Mixed Congregations*).

Comment: Every martyr knows how to save his/her life and yet refuses to do so. A public repudiation of the faith would save any of them. But some things are more precious than life itself. These martyrs prove that their twentieth-century countryman, C. S. Lewis, was correct in saying that courage is not simply one of the virtues but the form (shape) of every virtue at the testing point, that is, at the point of highest reality.

Blessed Angeline of Marsciano (III)
1374-1435

Blessed Angeline founded the first community of Franciscan women other than Poor Clares to receive papal approval.

Angeline was born to the Duke of Marsciano (near Orvieto). She was twelve when her mother died. Three years later the young woman made a vow of perpetual chastity. That same year, however, she yielded to her father's decision that she marry the Duke of Civitella. Her husband agreed to respect her previous vow.

When he died two years later, Angeline joined the Secular Franciscans and with several other women dedicated herself to caring for the sick, the poor, widows and orphans. When many other young women were attracted to Angeline's community, some people accused her of condemning the married vocation.

Legend has it that when she came before the king of Naples to answer these charges, she had burning coals hidden in the folds of her cloak. When she proclaimed her innocence and showed the king that these coals had not harmed her, he dropped the case.

Angeline and her companions later went to Foligno, where her community of Third Order sisters received papal approval in 1397. She soon established fifteen similar communities of women in other Italian cities.

Angeline died on July 14, 1435, and was beatified in 1825.

Quote: Pope Paul VI wrote in 1971: "Without in any way undervaluing human love and marriage — is not the latter, according to faith, the image and sharing of the union of love joining Christ and the Church? — consecrated chastity evokes this union in a more immediate way and brings that surpassing excellence to which all human love should tend" (*Apostolic Exhortation on the Renewal of Religious Life*, #13).

Comment: Priests, sisters and brothers cannot be signs of God's love for the human family if they belittle the vocation of marriage. Angeline respected marriage but felt called to another way of living out the gospel. Her choice was life-giving in its own way.

Saint Francis Solano (I)
1549-1610

Francis came from a leading family in Andalusia, Spain. Perhaps it was his popularity as a student that enabled Francis in his teens to stop two duelists. He entered the Friars Minor in 1570, and after ordination enthusiastically sacrificed himself for others. His care for the sick during an epidemic drew so much admiration that he became embarrassed and asked to be sent to the African missions. Instead he was sent to South America in 1589.

While working in what is now Argentina, Bolivia and Paraguay, Francis quickly learned the local languages and was well received by the indigenous peoples. His visits to the sick often included playing a song on his violin.

Around 1601 he was called to Lima, Peru, where he tried to recall the Spanish colonists to their baptismal integrity. Francis also worked to defend the indigenous peoples from oppression. He died in Lima and was canonized in 1726.

Quote: "When Francis Solano was about to die, one of the friars asked him, 'Father, when God takes you to heaven remember me when you enter the everlasting kingdom.' With joy Francis answered, 'It is true, I am going to heaven but this is so because of the merits of the passion and death of Christ; I am the greatest of sinners. When I reach our homeland, I will be your good friend'" (contemporary biography of Saint Francis Solano).

Comment: Francis of Solano knew from experience that the lives of Christians sometimes greatly hinder the spread of the gospel of Jesus Christ. Francis lived an exemplary life himself, and urged his fellow Spaniards to make their lives worthy of their Baptism.

Saint Bonaventure (I)
1218-1274

Bonaventure was born at Bagnoregio in Tuscany and was baptized John. As a child he was cured by Saint Francis. Bonaventure studied at the University of Paris and became a Franciscan there. At the same time Thomas Aquinas was teaching at Paris, Bonaventure was a distinguished teacher there.

His academic career was cut short by his election as minister general of the friars in 1257. Bonaventure immediately dedicated his energies to restoring harmony among the friars, who were plagued by various factions.

The Church in the 1260's closely linked ordination and the permission to preach. This presented a problem for the friars whose style, since Francis' time, had been that of itinerant preachers — few of whom were ordained. Bonaventure, wanting to insure the friars' preaching vocation, moved them in a clerical direction. And accepting ordination meant establishing large houses of study near universities like Paris and Oxford.

Though some people have criticized Bonaventure for this redirection of the friars, others have argued convincingly that he was simply following the mind of the Church — which, they say, is what Francis would have wanted. Bonaventure ably defended the friars against those who said that the friars' form of life, with its provision for begging, was condemned by the gospel.

Among Bonaventure's most famous writings are his life of Saint Francis (*Legenda Major*) and the equally brilliant *Journey of the Soul to God*. Bonaventure attributed his knowledge to meditation on the cross.

Bonaventure worked hard not to be named a bishop but was finally made Bishop of Albano and then cardinal. At the Second Council of Lyons (1274), he worked for reunion with the Greek Church. He died before the council ended. Bonaventure was canonized in 1482.

Quote: "In this passing over, if it is to be perfect, all intellectual activities must be left behind and the height of our affection must be totally transferred and transformed into God. This, however, is mystical and most secret, which no one knows except him who receives it, no one receives except him who desires it, and no one desires except him who is inflamed in his very marrow by the fire of the Holy Spirit whom Christ sent into the world. And therefore the Apostle says that this mystical wisdom is revealed by the Holy Spirit" (Bonaventure: *The Soul's Journey Into God*, chapter seven).

Comment: Bonaventure's goal was "wisdom" — knowledge in the light of faith. His various publics — students, friars, Church officials — knew him as a man who fulfilled the Franciscan educational motto: In holiness and learning.

Like Saint Francis, Bonaventure knew that poverty and humility are the natural allies of the gospel.

July 17

Francisco Garcés and Companions (I)
d. 1781

Government interference in the missions and landgrabbing sparked the Indian uprising which cost these friars their lives.

A contemporary of the American Revolution and of Junipero Serra (July 1), Francisco Garcés was born in 1738 in Spain, where he joined the Franciscans. After ordination in 1763, he was sent to Mexico. Five years later he was assigned to San Xavier del Bac near Tucson, one of several missions the Jesuits had founded in Arizona and New Mexico before being expelled in 1767 from all territories controlled by the Catholic king of Spain. In Arizona, Francisco worked among the Papago, Yuma, Pima and Apache Native Americans. His missionary travels took him to the Grand Canyon and to California.

Friar Francisco Palou, a contemporary, writes that Father Garcés was greatly loved by the indigenous peoples, among whom he lived unharmed for a long time. They regularly gave him food and referred to him as *"Viva Jesus,"* which was the greeting he taught them to use.

For the sake of their indigenous converts, the Spanish missionaries wanted to organize settlements away from the Spanish soldiers and colonists. But the commandant in Mexico insisted that two new missions on the Colorado River, Misión San Pedro y San Pablo and Misión La Purísima Concepción, be mixed settlements.

A revolt among the Yumas against the Spanish left Friars Juan Diaz and Matias Moreno dead at Misión San Pedro y San Pablo. Friars Francisco Garcés and Juan Barreneche were killed at Misión La Purísima Concepción (the site of Fort Yuma).

Quote: On a visit to Africa in 1969, Pope Paul VI told twenty-two young Ugandan converts that "being a Christian is a fine thing but not always an easy one."

Comment: In the eighteenth century the indigenous peoples of the American Southwest saw Catholicism and Spanish rule as a package deal. When they wanted to throw off the latter, the new religion had to go also. Do we appreciate sufficiently the acceptable adjustment our faith can make among various peoples? Are we offended by the customs of Catholics in other cultures? Do we see our good example as a contribution to missionary evangelization?

July 21

Saint Lawrence of Brindisi (I)
1559-1619

Saint Francis wanted his followers to preach what they had learned in prayer. Lawrence was an excellent example of this.

Lawrence was born of devout middle-class parents in Brindisi in southern Italy. He entered the Capuchins at the age of sixteen and proved an able scholar with a gift for languages. His ability to preach in five languages was put to good use after his ordination in 1582. When Lawrence preached, he used Scripture extensively. His sermons fill eight large volumes.

His career falls into three main categories: teaching theology to the friars, serving as an occasional papal diplomat, and holding various leadership positions within the Capuchins. In the last role he sought to balance the rigors of the Capuchin observance with the needs of the apostolate.

During his lifetime, Lawrence was the provincial of three different Italian provinces. He was a general definitor (councillor) twice and vicar general once. In 1598 he and thirteen other friars went to Germany to establish the Capuchins there; three provinces in time grew from their mission.

In 1601, Lawrence accompanied the imperial troops that repelled the Turkish advance in Hungary. On returning to Italy, Lawrence learned of a cruel viceroy in Naples, which was ruled by Spain. When Lawrence journeyed to Lisbon to explain the situation to Philip III of Spain, the viceroy was dismissed. Lawrence died in Lisbon on that journey.

After Lawrence's death a preacher said of him: "Heroically virtuous, he was humble without littleness, magnanimous without ostentation, courageous without pride. His faith would have moved mountains, his hope defied every trial, and his charity knew no bounds. He united the life of action with the life of contemplation, so that he gave himself up to incessant labors for the defense of the Church and the salvation of his neighbor, and yet never lost sight of the holy presence of the Divine majesty."

Lawrence was canonized in 1881 and declared a Doctor of the Church in 1958.

Quote: "The word of God is a light to the mind and fire to the will. It enables man to know God and to love him. And for the interior man who lives by the Spirit of God through grace, it is bread and water, but a bread sweeter than honey and the honeycomb, a water better than wine and milk" (Saint Lawrence, *Sermo Quadragesimalis* 2).

Comment: Lawrence was an effective preacher because his life affirmed his sermons. Truly great preaching requires a basis of prayer and penance.

July 24

Blessed Modestino of Jesus and Mary (I)
1802-1854

Born in 1802 near Naples, he joined the Friars Minor in 1822 and was ordained five years later. After twelve years as a noted preacher, confessor and exemplary guardian in two friaries, he was transferred to Santa Maria della Sanità, a very poor section of Naples and his home for the next fourteen years.

His concern for the newborn, the sick and the poor inspired generosity on the part of wealthier Neapolitans. He died in 1854 while ministering to cholera victims. He was beatified in 1995.

Quote: In his beatification homily, Pope John Paul II said: "Father Modestino lived in a society of marginalization and moral suffering, and was able to share fully the expectations and anxieties of the weakest, responding to the deep need for God found in his brothers and sisters who thirsted for justice and love. He thus became a leaven of renewal and a living sign of hope. The hand of the Lord was truly upon him, making him a minister of mercy and comfort to every class, especially through his diligent, patient celebration of the sacrament of Reconciliation" (1995 LOR 5:1).

Comment: Saintly people always challenge us — not to imitate them slavishly but to live out our baptismal calling as generously as they lived theirs. Modestino touched the consciences of wealthy Neapolitans and prompted them to see poor people not as nuisances but as their sisters and brothers in Christ. Celebrating the Sacrament of Reconciliation regularly helps us form a good conscience.

July 25

Blessed Antonio Lucci
1682-1752

Antonio studied with and was a friend of Saint Francesco Antonio Fasani (November 27), who after Antonio Lucci's death testified at the diocesan hearings regarding the holiness of Lucci.

Born in Agnone in southern Italy, a city famous for manufacturing bells and copper crafts, he was given the name Angelo in baptism. He attended the local school run by the Conventuals and joined them at the age of sixteen. Antonio completed his studies for ordination in Assisi, where he was ordained in 1705. Further studies led to a doctorate in theology and appointments as a teacher in Agnone, Ravello and Naples. He also served as guardian in Naples.

Elected minister provincial in 1718, the following year he was appointed professor at St. Bonaventure College in Rome, a position he held until Pope Benedict XIII chose him as bishop of Bovino (near Foggia) in 1729. The pope explained, "I have chosen as bishop of Bovino an eminent theologian and a great saint."

His twenty-three years as bishop were marked by visits to local parishes and a renewal of gospel living among the people of his diocese. He dedicated his episcopal income to works of education and charity. At the urging of the Conventual minister general, Bishop Lucci wrote a major book about the saints and blesseds in the first two hundred years of the Conventual Franciscans.

He was beatified in 1989, three years after his friend Francesco Antonio Fasani was canonized.

Quote: When Francis of Assisi learned that Anthony of Padua was teaching theology to the friars in Bologna, Francis wrote: "It pleases me that you teach sacred theology to the brothers, as long as — in the words of the Rule — you do not extinguish the spirit of prayer and devotion with study of this kind."

Comment: Franciscan teachers have tried to observe this command, encouraging their students to let their studies stimulate their prayer and support their spiritual growth as well as their apostolic work. Antonio Lucci was such a teacher. As Pope Paul VI wrote in 1975, people today "are more impressed by witnesses than by teachers, and if they listen to these it is because they also bear witness" (*Evangelization in the Modern World*, #41).

July 30

Saint Leopold Mandic of Castelnova (I)
1887-1942

Western Christians who are working for greater dialogue with Orthodox Christians may be reaping the fruits of Father Leopold's prayers.

A native of Croatia, Leopold joined the Capuchins and was ordained several years later in spite of several health problems. He could not speak loudly enough to preach publicly. For many years he also suffered from severe arthritis, poor eyesight and a stomach ailment.

Leopold taught patrology, the study of the Church Fathers, to the clerics of his province for several years, but he is best known for his work in the confessional, where he sometimes spent thirteen to fifteen hours a day. Several bishops sought out his spiritual advice.

Leopold's dream was to go to the Orthodox Christians and work for the reunion of Roman Catholicism and Orthodoxy. His health never permitted it. Leopold often renewed his vow to go to the Eastern Christians; the cause of unity was constantly in his prayers.

At a time when Pope Pius XII said that the greatest sin of our time is "to have lost all sense of sin," Leopold had a profound sense of sin and an even firmer sense of God's grace awaiting human cooperation.

Leopold, who lived most of his life in Padua, died on July 30, 1942, and was canonized in 1982.

Quote: Leopold used to repeat to himself: "Remember that you have been sent for the salvation of people, not because of your own merits, since it is the Lord Jesus and not you who died for the salvation of souls.... I must cooperate with the divine goodness of our Lord who has deigned to choose me so that by my ministry, the divine promise would be fulfilled: 'So there will be one flock, one shepherd' (John 10:16)."

Comment: Saint Francis advised his followers to "pursue what they must desire above all things, to have the Spirit of the Lord and His holy manner of working" (*Rule of 1223*, Chapter 10) — words that Leopold lived out. When the Capuchin minister general wrote his friars on the occasion of Leopold's beatification, he said that this friar's life showed "the priority of that which is essential."

August 2

Dedication of the Chapel of Our Lady of the Angels (Portiuncula)

Francis rebuilt this chapel with his own hands and died less than fifty feet away from it.

The chapel of Our Lady of the Angels, down the hill from the walled city of Assisi, was built out of devotion but had deteriorated by the time of Francis' conversion (1206). Although it belonged to the Benedictine monks on nearby Mount Subasio, few people then lived close to the Portiuncula, "Mary's little portion."

After having rebuilt the small churches of San Damiano and later San Pietro, which no longer exists, Francis rebuilt this chapel. In time it would be called the "cradle of Franciscanism," important to the friars, the Poor Clares and the Secular Franciscans.

While attending Mass here one day, Francis heard a reading from the Gospel of Matthew in which Jesus sends out the apostles without gold, silver, money, not carrying a traveling bag, food or a walking staff and not wearing sandals or having two tunics; instead they should preach the kingdom of God and penance. Francis exclaimed, "This is what I wish, this is what I seek, this is what I long to do with all my heart" (*1 Celano*, #22).

A few years later, Francis and the other friars received the Lady Clare here on Palm Sunday evening (1212), gave her a religious garb and cut her hair as a sign of entrance into a new way of life. The Benedictines gave Francis the chapel, which soon became his headquarters; here the friars assembled in annual chapters to report on what they had accomplished with God's grace and to decide on new territories for evangelizing. Here Francis resigned in 1221 as minister general of the friars. Because this chapel had a special role in Francis' conversion, it became a place very special to members of the Secular Franciscan Order. A few feet from this chapel, Francis died just after sunset on October 3, 1226.

By that time, Francis had gained from Pope Honorius III the "Pardon of Assisi," a plenary indulgence, under the usual conditions of prayer, confession and reception of the Eucharist, for everyone who visited this small chapel on the anniversary of its dedication (August 2). In 1569 construction began on the basilica which now surrounds the chapel. The hillside city of Assisi has stopped growing geographically; expansion now occurs on the plain near Our Lady of the Angels Basilica.

Thousands of pilgrims come here every year to pray for their own intentions, for family needs and for reconciliation throughout the world. On October 27, 1986, Pope John Paul II and two hundred and thirty-five leaders of the world's major religions began their Day of Prayer for World Peace with a prayer service in front of this tiny chapel.

Quote: On that Day of Prayer for World Peace, Pope John Paul II said at the Portiuncula: "I have chosen this town of Assisi as the place for our Day of Prayer for Peace because of the particular significance of the holy man venerated here — Saint Francis — known and revered by so many throughout the world as a symbol of peace, reconciliation and brotherhood. Inspired by his example, his meekness and humility, let us dispose our hearts for prayer in true internal silence."

Comment: In this chapel, Francis of Assisi began to understand more about the truth of his life, his service of God and how both of those are connected to service of other people. Truth and forgiveness provide the only lasting foundations for genuine peace.

Blessed Frédéric Janssoone (I)
1838-1916

Frédéric's openness to God's grace included a couple of seeming detours, travels in several countries and a life that drew his contemporaries to God.

Born near Lille (France) in 1838, Frédéric lost his father at the age of ten. Frédéric entered the seminary but then left in order to support his mother. For several years he worked as a traveling salesperson before joining the Friars Minor. After his ordination in 1870, he served as a military chaplain and then ministered for five years in the Holy Land.

Sent to Canada in 1881, he collected alms for the Holy Land Custody. A year later Frédéric returned to the Holy Land for six more years of service. Transferred back to Canada in 1888, he was instrumental in reestablishing the Montreal-based province of the Friars Minor. A man of deep prayer and great apostolic zeal, he made his headquarters at the Shrine of Our Lady at Cap-de-la-Madeleine near Trois-Rivières. Pilgrimages and reports of miracles at that parish church soon made it a national shrine. He assisted the Poor Clare monastery in Valleyfield and was widely known for his parish missions, promotion of the Secular Franciscan Order and his literary activities.

He died in Montreal, but was buried at his beloved Trois-Rivières. He was beatified in 1988.

Quote: In his beatification homily, Pope John Paul II said: "A true son of St. Francis, Father Frédéric gives us the example of contemplative prayer, which is able to embrace the works of creation, the events of daily life, and encounters with each person. ...He taught his contemporaries to be consistent and ardent witnesses of the Gospel" (1988 LOR 43:15).

Comment: Faithful prayer was the power behind "Bon Père Frédéric's" zealous apostolic work. Union with God in prayer enabled Frédéric to announce the Good News of Jesus Christ on three continents "whether the time is favorable or unfavorable" (2 Timothy 4:2).

Saint John Vianney (III)
1786-1859

A diocesan priest and Secular Franciscan who humbly accepted an assignment to a village of indifferent Catholics is today the patron of all diocesan priests!

Remembered today simply as the Curé of Ars, John Vianney was born three years before the start of the French Revolution of devout farming parents in Dardilly. Because of the revolutionary anti-Catholic fervor, the Vianney family had to attend Mass in secret.

Studies were never easy for John. His early education was cut short by the need for his work on the farm. When he wanted to become a priest, his father was opposed but eventually consented. In 1809, John was drafted to serve in Napoleon's army. He deserted the next year and hid in Le Noes, a mountain town. That same year Napoleon granted amnesty to all military deserters so John resumed his studies and was ordained in 1815.

In 1818, he was assigned to the village of Ars, where religious practice was very weak. Diocesan priests considered such an assignment a punishment. His solitary prayer before the Blessed Sacrament helped convince the villagers that John was not like the two previous pastors who had left the priesthood. His asceticism, which could not be completely concealed, also helped win the people over. At the beginning of the week, he would boil a pot of potatoes; that was his main food for the week.

Neglect of Sunday Mass and of catechetical instructions were corrected within a few years. The excessive drinking for which Ars had become famous gradually subsided. The people grew to love their pastor. In fact, the first time John was assigned to another town, the parishioners persuaded the bishop to let him stay!

John eventually spent sixteen to eighteen hours a day hearing confessions. As many as twenty thousand people came in a single year to visit Ars and to confess to him. Broken by his work and his penances, John died on August 4, 1859. He was canonized in 1925 and was later named patron of all diocesan priests.

Quote: John Vianney once said, "I have been privileged to give great gifts from my empty hands."

Comment: Lesser men might have tried to attribute such confessional fame to themselves, but John's works of penance helped keep his priorities clear. He regularly confessed his sins. The practice helped him to see more clearly the truth about God, himself and others — in short, to be humble. Because of this, God could accomplish great things through him.

Ignatius Brady (I)
1911-1990

Ignatius the scholar lived out Francis' command to Anthony of Padua that studies should never extinguish the spirit of prayer and devotion.

Born in Detroit, Charles studied for five years in the archdiocesan seminary. His interest in Francis of Assisi led him to become a friar, making his first profession in 1930; he was ordained seven years later. After obtaining a doctorate in philosophy, he taught for ten years at Duns Scotus College outside Detroit. He taught at several other colleges and universities, including two years at Catholic University of America in Washington, D.C.

Ignatius helped lay the solid foundation for a renewal in Franciscan spirituality in the 1950's as well as during and after Vatican II. In the 1950's and 1970's he taught at the Franciscan Institute, part of St. Bonaventure University near Allegany, New York. He frequently gave retreats and workshops to friars, Poor Clares and many congregations of Franciscan sisters around the world. He helped general chapters of men and women Franciscans to refocus their energies, making their Franciscan charism the leaven of their apostolic work and community living. He was chaplain for the Franciscan Missionaries of Mary in Grottaferrata.

Cardinal John Wright once described Ignatius as a "renowned scholar, a spiritual director, an intellectual with a strong pastoral sense and a great gentleman." Ignatius enlivened many gatherings with a well-chosen song or funny story.

For many years Ignatius headed the theological section of the Friars Minor research institute, located first at Quaracchi (near Florence) and later in Grottaferrata (near Rome). He produced seven critical editions of scholarly works, six books, seven translations and forty-three scholarly articles. Many students of Franciscan studies turned to "Iggy" for advice in completing their doctoral dissertations. He willingly and humbly shared his expertise, always as a true Friar Minor.

Quote: Ignatius wrote: "Francis was 'ever new' (2 *Celano*, 159) and ever seeking new insights into the ways of God in the hearts of the pure and simple.... On their part, the friars soon learned that Francis was a man of the Spirit, that the Spirit of the Lord rested in him with great fulness, since he was able to read their hearts and direct their own spirits along the ways of God" (1 *Celano*, #48, cited in Ignatius Brady, O.F.M., "St. Francis and the Holy Spirit," *Sursum Corda* 14:5, pages 217-218).

Comment: The Good News of Jesus was always fresh in the life of Ignatius. Students, retreatants, confreres, friends and family members benefitted from his prayer, self-sacrifice and humble learning.

August 6

Venerable Anthony Margil (I)
1657-1726

Anthony was born in Valencia, Spain. After he joined the Franciscans and was ordained, he decided to become a missionary. When the missionary college of Santa Cruz in Querétaro, Mexico, was organized, Anthony volunteered and was accepted. In 1683 he arrived in Vera Cruz and found that city had been devastated by a pirate attack. Life in the New World would not be easy.

Anthony covered a wide territory in his forty-three years in New Spain. He worked in Costa Rica, Guatemala, Mexico and Texas. After serving as superior in Querétaro for thirteen years, he established missionary colleges in Guatemala City and in Zacatecas, Mexico.

Although Anthony was used to self-denial, missionary life provided plenty of mortification. He walked thousands of miles and showed great courage among hostile Indians.

In 1716 missionaries from the Zacatecas college founded Misión Guadalupe in eastern Texas. Anthony himself established the missions of Dolores and San Miguel in that state. When war with Spain caused the French to invade east Texas in 1719, Anthony and his confreres withdrew to Misión San Antonio (later known as the Alamo), which had been set up the previous year. In 1720, he began Misión San José in San Antonio.

Anthony died in Mexico City on August 6, 1726. In 1836 he was declared venerable.

Quote: "But before all this occurs, they will arrest you and persecute you; they will hand you over to synagogues and prisons, and you will be brought before kings and governors because of my name.... So make up your minds not to prepare your defense in advance; for I will give you words and a wisdom which none of your opponents will be able to withstand or contradict" (Luke 21:12, 14-15).

Comment: Missionaries like Anthony have difficult lives. Their work is often hard, and its fruit not often apparent. Like missionaries before him and since then, Anthony trusted that God would ultimately bring some good out of all these sacrifices.

August 9

Mother Marianne of Molokai (III)
1838-1918

Though leprosy scared off most people in nineteenth-century Hawaii, that disease sparked great generosity in Mother Marianne. Her courage helped tremendously to improve the lives of its victims in Hawaii, a territory annexed to the United States during her lifetime (1898).

On January 23, 1838, a daughter was born to Peter and Barbara Cope of Hessen-Darmstadt, Germany. The girl was named after her mother. Two years later the Cope family emigrated to the United States and settled in Utica, New York. Young Barbara worked in a factory until August 1862, when she went to the Sisters of the Third Order of Saint Francis in Syracuse, New York. After profession in November of the next year, she began teaching at Assumption parish school.

Marianne held the post of superior in several places and was twice the novice mistress of her congregation. A natural leader, three different times she was superior of St. Joseph's Hospital in Syracuse, where she learned much that would be useful during her years in Hawaii.

Elected provincial in 1877, Mother Marianne was unanimously re-elected in 1881. Two years later the Hawaiian government was searching for someone to run the Kakaako Receiving Station for people suspected of having leprosy. More than fifty religious communities in the United States and Canada were asked. When the request was put to the Syracuse sisters, thirty-five of them volunteered immediately. On October 22, 1883, Mother Marianne and six other sisters left for Hawaii where they took charge of the Kakaako Receiving Station outside Honolulu; on the island of Maui they also opened a hospital and a school for girls.

In 1888, Mother Marianne and two sisters went to Molokai to open a home for "unprotected women and girls" there. The Hawaiian government was quite hesitant to send women for this difficult assignment; they need not have worried about Mother Marianne! On Molokai she took charge of the home that Blessed Damien DeVeuster (d. 1889) had established for men and boys. Mother Marianne changed life on Molokai by introducing cleanliness, pride and fun to the colony. Bright scarves and pretty dresses for the women were part of her approach.

Awarded the Royal Order of Kapiolani by the Hawaiian government and celebrated in a poem by Robert Louis Stevenson, Mother Marianne continued her work faithfully. Her sisters have attracted vocations among the Hawaiian people and still work on Molokai.

Mother Marianne died on August 9, 1918. Work leading to the introduction of her cause in Rome has begun.

Quote: Soon after Mother Marianne died, Mrs. John F. Bowler wrote in the *Honolulu Advertiser*: "Seldom has the opportunity come to a woman to devote every hour of 30 years to the mothering of people isolated by law from the rest of the world. She risked her own life in all that time, faced everything with unflinching courage and smiled sweetly through it all."

Comment: The government authorities were reluctant to allow Mother Marianne to be a mother on Molokai. Thirty years of dedication proved their fears unfounded. God grants gifts regardless of human short-sightedness and allows those gifts to flower for the sake of the kingdom.

August 11

Saint Clare of Assisi
Foundress of the Second Order
1193-1253

Clare became a light to the whole Church because she followed Jesus with all her strength.

Clare's parents, Favarone and Ortolana, were part of Assisi's nobility. They and their three daughters fled to nearby Perugia when the merchants and artisans of Assisi, including the family of the young Francis, expelled the nobles and destroyed their castles (1198-1202).

While still a young girl, Clare showed a love of prayer and of the poor. She was also fascinated by Francis Bernardone, who had eleven followers already in 1209. She felt called to live the gospel as a nun. On the evening of March 18, 1212, she stole away to the Portiuncula and there exchanged her beautiful golden hair for a nun's veil and her rich gown for a common dress and cord belt. She was soon joined by her sister Agnes (November 19), and they lived temporarily with nearby Benedictine sisters.

In May of that year, Clare and Agnes moved to San Damiano which soon became the birthplace of the Poor Clare movement. Officially they were known as the "Poor Ladies of San Damiano." The work of their hands and the begging of the friars supplied their modest needs.

In 1216, Clare reluctantly accepted the title of abbess in accord with the Fourth Lateran Council. She did not stand on that title, however, and was always ready to perform the humblest duties at San Damiano. After 1225 she was almost constantly sick and confined to bed. With great devotion she made corporals and altar linens for nearby churches.

Though Clare considered herself the "little plant" of Saint Francis and was always grateful for whatever direction he could give the nuns at San Damiano, it would be a mistake to think of Clare as a pale reflection of Francis or to underestimate her uniqueness and her determination to live the gospel simply and courageously within a cloistered setting.

In the thirteenth century, the contemplative life was the only form of religious life for women that was officially recognized by the Church. Women religious would not run schools and hospitals until the fourteenth and fifteenth centuries. Even though Clare established a contemplative group, she did break with tradition — not without a fight — by rejecting a fixed income for its support. Contemplative nuns had always been supported by revenues from lands owned by their communities and by the dowries they brought with them.

Gaining — in writing — the "privilege of poverty," as Clare called it, was no easy task. Several popes worried that such a life would be too difficult for women. Two days before she died, Clare at last gained this "privilege" from Pope Innocent IV.

Clare had a keen sense of the Mystical Body of Christ; she knew that the nuns at San Damiano were connected to every other part of the Church. Her example prompted rich and poor women throughout Europe to join Poor Clare monasteries. Popes and bishops sought her advice.

She was canonized in 1255, two years after her death.

Quote: As Clare lay dying, her confessor urged her to be patient amid her many sufferings. Clare answered, "Dearest brother, ever since I have known the grace of my Lord Jesus Christ through his servant Francis, no suffering has troubled me, no penance has been hard, no sickness too arduous" (Ignatius Brady, O.F.M., *The Legend and Writings of St. Clare of Assisi*, page 49).

Comment: According to Father Lothar Hardick, O.F.M., Clare's virtues "were not special gifts of grace alone; they were also gifts of nature. Following the guidance of Francis, she regarded all her natural talents and capacities as precious endowments to be used for the honor and glory of God. She made no attempt to crush them, but rather cooperated with the power of grace to perfect them" (Ignatius Brady, O.F.M., *The Legend and Writings of St. Clare of Assisi*, page 137).

August 14

Saint Maximilian Kolbe (I)
1894-1941

An offer to exchange places with a condemned man was the final self-sacrifice of a life filled with generosity.

Raymond Kolbe was born in Zdunska-Vola, Poland. He and his brother Francis went to the Conventual Franciscan seminary in Lvív. Raymond entered the friars and took the name Maximilian. For seven years he studied philosophy and theology in Rome. While there Maximilian established the Knights of Mary Immaculate, an organization dedicated to recognizing Mary as the Queen and Mother of human society and God's instrument for the conversion of the world. Maximilian was ordained in 1918.

Despite ill health, in 1927 he established Niepokalanow (City of the Immaculate) near Warsaw. This grew to be a huge Franciscan community (738 members) engaged in printing religious publications, the largest of which, *Knight of Mary Immaculate*, had a circulation of almost one million. The fantastic growth of this apostolate occurred during the worst years of the worldwide depression in the 1930's. During most of that decade, Maximilian was establishing another City of the Immaculate near Nagasaki, Japan.

He returned to Poland before World War II began. The Nazis restricted his activities severely and then halted publication of the *Knight* in December 1940. He was arrested the following February and sent to Auschwitz in May. Though very sick himself, he encouraged his fellow prisoners not to let the Nazis cause them to despair of God.

Dr. Joseph Stemler, another prisoner, remembers: "Like many others, I crawled at night in the infirmary on the bare floor to the bed of Father Maximilian. The greeting was moving. We exchanged some impressions of the frightful crematorium. He encouraged me, and I confessed. Discouragement and doubt threatened to overwhelm me; but I still wanted to love. He helped me to strengthen my belief in the final victory of good. 'Hatred is not creative,' he whispered to me. 'Our sorrow is necessary that those who live after may be happy.' His reflections on the mercy of God went straight to my heart. His words to forgive the persecutors and to overcome evil with good kept me from collapsing into despair."

On July 30, 1941, when a prisoner escaped from Auschwitz, the Nazis retaliated by randomly selecting ten men to starve to death. Father Maximilian offered to take the place of Sergeant Francis Gajowniczek, one of those ten. In their starvation bunker, Maximilian led the men in prayer. During the third week, the camp executioner killed Maximilian and the other three survivors with injections of carbolic acid.

Maximilian's cell at Auschwitz has become a place of pilgrimage. He was canonized in 1982.

Quote: Father Maximilian wrote to one of the friars: "Dear brother, see the greatness of man's dignity conferred by God's mercy. By obedience we surmount, so to speak, the limits imposed upon us by our weakness; we are made conformable to God's will which in his infinite wisdom and prudence guides us to act correctly. As a matter of fact by clinging to God's will — and no creature can resist it — we surpass everything in power. This is the way of wisdom and prudence; this is the only way we can render the greatest glory to God. If there were another and more suitable way, Christ surely would have showed it to us by his own words and example."

Comment: The most peaceful people sometimes die tragically at the hands of the violent; thus Maximilian Kolbe died. On his 1979 visit to Poland, Pope John Paul II called Auschwitz "a place built on hatred and contempt for man in the name of crazed ideology." The pope said that at Auschwitz Maximilian Kolbe won a victory "through faith and love."

Mother Maria Maddalena Bentivoglio (II)
1834-1905

When the United States was celebrating the hundredth anniversary of the Declaration of Independence, the Poor Clares had not yet made a permanent foundation in this country. Maddalena Bentivoglio was, however, about to change that.

Anna Maria was the twelfth child of Domenico and Angela Sandri Bentivoglio. Annetta — as she was nicknamed — was not a child saint. At her first boarding school, she was well known to the disciplinarian. Raised in Rome, Annetta soon grew familiar with St. Peter's, the Vatican and the Colosseum. Once, when the family was at St. Peter's for a special ceremony and she had been left at home, Anna Maria got into the church through a back way and inched her way along a ledge high above the main floor to watch the event!

Her father was an official in the Papal States. A revolution in 1848 sent Pope Pius IX and the Bentivoglio family into a two-year exile. In 1865 Annetta joined the Poor Clares at San Lorenzo, the community to which her sister Costanza already belonged. Annetta took the name Maria Maddalena of the Sacred Heart of Jesus. Though a modified form of the Rule of Saint Clare was observed at San Lorenzo, Maddalena and Costanza soon became interested in following the primitive Rule of Saint Clare.

In 1874 Mother Ignatius Hayes (May 6), a Third Order sister from Minnesota, came to Italy to seek candidates for a community she was establishing at Belle Prairie, Minnesota. Pope Pius IX gave permission to Maddalena and Costanza to set up a Poor Clare house in that state; he also sent a Franciscan priest as their spiritual director. Once they arrived in New York, however, the spiritual director decided not to go to Minnesota. The sisters wrote to the Franciscan minister general for instructions. He advised finding a bishop willing to have a Poor Clare monastery in his diocese; if that failed, they should return to Italy.

Turned down by the archbishop of New York, the sisters made unsuccessful attempts to establish monasteries first in Philadelphia and then in New Orleans. In August 1877, Maddalena and three companions (two recruits from New Orleans) arrived in Cleveland, where they did establish a monastery that included several Colletine Poor Clares from Harreveld, Netherlands. The next year Maddalena and Costanza went to Omaha, Nebraska, where with the generous help of John Creighton they began building a monastery in 1880. Internal dissensions led to several canonical investigations which ultimately cleared Maddalena (abbess) and Costanza (vicaress) of all wrongdoing.

Foundations in New Orleans (1885) and Evansville, Indiana (1897), helped put to rest any doubts as to whether the contemplative life could attract vocations in America. Mother Maddalena died in Evansville on August 18, 1905. Her cause has been introduced in Rome.

Quote: "It is courage that makes the saint; and courage is no more than confidence in grace that comes from on high and is always available, though we do not always open our hearts to receive it" (Louis Lavelle, *Four Saints*).

Comment: Mother Mary Maddalena was certainly a courageous woman. At a time when some U.S. bishops were skeptical of or hostile to the establishment of Poor Clare monasteries in the United States, she had a strong sense of God's work for her. There will always be a great need for Franciscan sisters in hospitals, orphanages, homes for the aged, schools, parishes and the missions. Certainly there will always be a need for the charism of Saint Clare and of her spiritual daughters.

August 19

Saint Louis of Toulouse (I)
1274-1297

When he died at the age of twenty-three, Louis was already a Franciscan, a bishop and a saint!

Louis's parents were Charles II of Naples and Sicily and Mary, daughter of the king of Hungary. Louis was related to Saint Louis IX (August 25) on his father's side and to Elizabeth of Hungary (November 17) on his mother's side.

Louis showed early signs of attachment to prayer and to the corporal works of mercy. As a child he used to take food from the castle to feed the poor. When he was fourteen, Louis and two of his brothers were taken as hostages to the king of Aragon's court as part of a political deal involving Louis's father. At the court Louis was tutored by Franciscan friars under whom he made great progress both in his studies and in the spiritual life.

Like Saint Francis he developed a special love for those afflicted with leprosy.

While he was still a hostage, Louis decided to renounce his royal title and become a priest. When he was twenty, he was allowed to leave the king of Aragon's court. He renounced his title in favor of his brother Robert and was ordained the next year. Very shortly after, he was appointed bishop of Toulouse, but the pope agreed to Louis's request to become a Franciscan first.

The Franciscan spirit pervaded Louis. "Jesus Christ is all my riches; he alone is sufficient for me," Louis kept repeating. Even as a bishop he wore the Franciscan habit and sometimes begged. He assigned a friar to offer him correction — in public if necessary — and the friar did his job.

Louis's service to the Diocese of Toulouse was richly blessed. In no time he was considered a saint. Louis set aside seventy-five percent of his income as bishop to feed the poor and maintain churches. Each day he fed twenty-five poor people at his table.

Louis was canonized in 1317 by Pope John XXII, one of his former teachers.

Quote: "All the faithful were edified by the fervor of his devout celebration of Mass, the efficacy of his deep humility, his tender compassion, his upright life, the harmonious congruity in all his actions, words and bearing. Who without wonderment could look upon a most charming young man, the son of so mighty a king, outstanding for his generosity, raised to such dignity, renowned for his influence, preeminent for humility, living a life of such mortification, endowed with such wisdom, clothed in so poor a habit yet renowned for the charm of his discourse and a shining example of upright life?" (contemporary biography)

Comment: When Cardinal Hugolino, the future Pope Gregory IX, suggested to Francis that some of the friars would make fine bishops, Francis protested that they might lose some of their humility and simplicity if appointed to those positions. Those two virtues are needed everywhere in the Church, and Louis shows us how they can be lived out by bishops.

Saint Pius X (III)
1835-1914

In response to a movement led by Pope Innocent III, Saint Francis wrote several letters promoting devotion to the Eucharist. Seven hundred years later Pope Pius X would make the Eucharist even more accessible by lowering the age for First Communion.

Joseph Sarto was born into a poor but devout family in Riese near Venice. After his ordination in 1858, he took Leonard of Port Maurice (November 26) as his model for living and preaching; holy hours became a part of Joseph's life. He joined the Secular Franciscan Order while he was pastor in Salzano.

In 1884 he was made bishop of Mantua, where he devoted himself to the poor and helped promote the Catholic press. In 1892 he became patriarch of Venice and was elected pope eleven years later.

The program of Pius X was to renew all things in Christ. He lowered the age for First Communion and encouraged even daily Communion. In 1909 he established the Pontifical Biblical Institute, a move that links him even closer to Saint Francis since the Biblical Institute has helped to make Scripture better known and loved.

Always a simple man, Pius X sometimes found the customs of the papal court a penance. As pope he continued his generosity to the poor. He once said, "I was born poor, I have lived poor, and I wish to die poor."

Pius X was crushed by the outbreak of World War I, which he had worked very hard to prevent. He died August 20, 1914, and was canonized in 1954.

Quote: Ludwig von Pastor, historian of the popes, said of Pius X: "He was one of those chosen few men whose personality is irresistible. Everyone was moved by his simplicity and his angelic kindness. Yet it was something more that carried him into all hearts; and that 'something' is best defined by saying that all who were ever admitted to his presence had a deep conviction of being face-to-face with a saint. And the more one knows about him, the stronger the conviction becomes."

Comment: A humble person makes us feel at home; we tend to be "on edge" in the presence of proud people. Jesus' humility made him very approachable; we see the same dynamic in Pius X. His work for world peace remains a challenge for us.

Blanche of Castile (III)
1188-1252

Blanche built up the Body of Christ by being, among other things, a loving wife and mother.

Blanche's father, Alfonso VII of Castile, arranged for her to marry Louis VIII of France in 1200. She and Louis had twelve children, including Saint Louis IX (August 25). Although she had many duties, Blanche trained her children to be good Christians and good rulers. It is said that she told Louis IX, "I would rather see you dead at my feet than stained with mortal sin."

When her husband died in 1226, Blanche ruled as regent for the next eight years. During that time she proved herself a very capable administrator. She also fought the Albigensian heretics in southern France. In 1248 she resumed her role as regent when Louis went on crusade.

Blanche joined the Secular Franciscans early in life. At her death people called her "Blessed" though this title was never officially recognized by the Church.

Quote: "I beg you, therefore, with all possible respect, not to forget the Lord or turn away from His commandments by reason of the cares and preoccupations of this world.... And you should manifest such honor to the Lord among the people entrusted to you that every evening an announcement be made by a town crier or some other signal that praise and thanks may be given by all people to the all-powerful Lord God" (Saint Francis, *Letter to the Rulers of the Peoples*).

Comment: Francis' respect for all people included rulers. His age was at least as riddled with corruption, violence and intrigue among those in power as ours is. Yet often we are skeptical that any good can come from those who have political power. Blanche serves as an example of how the Franciscan charism may have an effect at every level of human life.

Saint Louis IX
Patron of the Secular Franciscan Order
1214-1270

Louis carried out the highest office in France in a thoroughly Franciscan way.

His mother, the saintly Blanche of Castile (August 23), trained Louis for a double duty: kingship in France and membership in the kingdom of heaven. Louis was crowned king at the age of twelve, though Blanche ruled as regent for several years. Franciscan friars were among his instructors; eventually he became a Secular Franciscan.

Louis fasted throughout Advent and every Friday. Louis was generous in founding hospitals, building churches and promoting learning. In the 1250's there was a controversy at the University of Paris regarding the Dominicans and Franciscans. The professors there resented the independent but immensely popular schools of the mendicants. Louis openly supported the friars; Bonaventure (July 15) and Aquinas were honored guests at his table.

In 1248-1254 Louis led a crusade to recover the Holy Land. He went through North Africa and captured Damietta in Egypt, but was soon taken prisoner. When he was to be ransomed, his captors added a condition: He must deny his faith. Louis refused, and they eventually gave in.

Louis's greatest achievement was to rule his kingdom in the light of the gospel. He always considered God's law superior to his own laws. Louis worked hard to improve the administration of justice in his kingdom. He maintained good relations with the other Christian rulers of his day; three times he was called upon to mediate peace between opposing rulers in Europe.

Louis was a good father to his eleven children. He was very concerned to teach them the dignity of their Baptism, even over the nobility of their birth.

He died on his second crusade (1267-70) and was canonized in 1297.

Quote: "This Council exhorts Christians, as citizens of both cities, to perform their duties faithfully in the spirit of the Gospel. It is a mistake to think that, because we have here no lasting city, but seek the city which is to come, we are entitled to evade our earthly responsibilities; this is to forget that because of our faith we are all the more bound to fulfil these responsibilities according to each one's proper vocation" (Vatican II, *Pastoral Constitution on the Church*, #43).

Comment: We rarely associate kings with the spirit of Saint Francis, but Louis IX shows us that the Poverello's ideals can work there also. In some ways, following the gospel must have occasionally looked to Louis like a disadvantage, but he considered his chosen path worth any apparent drawbacks.

Martin of Valencia (I)
1470-1534

W hen Martin was born, the Americas had not been discovered. When he died, they were the focal point of the Catholic Church's evangelization efforts.

Born in a little village in León, Juan Martin de Boil entered the friars at Mayorga in the province of Santiago, Spain. After ordination he was assigned to his hometown. In 1517, the same year Martin Luther came to public notice in Germany, Martin de Boil became provincial of St. Gabriel Province of the Strict Observance.

In novitiate Martin, in imitation of Saint Francis, had begun to conform his life to that of Christ. But he did not realize his early desire to go to the missions until he was fifty-four years old.

In 1524, at the request of Emperor Charles V, Martin led eleven other friars to Mexico where they were eventually called "the twelve Apostles of Mexico." All of those early friars in Mexico were very poor and very penitential. On behalf of their indigenous converts, these friars protested injustices committed by the Spanish colonists.

Despite poor health, Martin was able to travel widely and through an interpreter explain the faith to the people he encountered. He died on one of his missionary journeys.

Quote: "The special end of this missionary activity is the evangelization and the implanting of the church among peoples and groups in which it has not yet taken root. All over the world indigenous particular churches ought to grow from the seed of the word of God, churches which would be adequately organized and would possess their own proper strength and maturity" (Vatican II, *Missionary Activity of the Church*, #6).

Comment: Over the years, spreading the Good News about Jesus has been identified as a task mostly for priests and religious. If in fact evangelization is "the deepest identity of the Church" as Pope Paul VI said, then this work rests to some degree on all members of the Church. Martin of Valencia's work is over; ours is not.

September 1

Saint Beatrice of Silva (II)
1424-1491

Beatrice has a slim but significant connection to the Franciscan movement. The Order she founded was not incorporated into the Franciscans until after her death but is today a major branch of the Franciscan family.

Beatrice was born in Ceuta, Morocco. She was related to the Portuguese royal family and served for a time as a lady-in-waiting to the queen of Castile. Leaving that position, she went to a Dominican convent in Toledo, where she lived (though she never took the vows of that Order) for thirty-seven years.

Seven years before her death, Beatrice established a contemplative community that observed the Cistercian Rule. Three years after her death, Pope Alexander VI placed her community under the Observant Friars Minor and gave it the Rule of Saint Clare. These nuns are now known as the Conceptionist Poor Clares and by 1968 formed almost twenty percent of the Second Order. Beatrice was canonized in 1976.

Quote: Celano wrote of the early followers of Francis, "For above everything else there flourishes among them that excelling virtue of mutual and continual charity, which so binds their wills into one that, though forty or fifty of them dwell together in one place, agreement in likes and dislikes molds one spirit in them out of many" (1 *Celano*, #19).

Comment: Some people are awed by the prayer and penances of the Poor Clares. Others are inspired by the charity and self-sacrifice required to keep such a community faithful to its goal: serving the Lord and his Church in greater and greater purity of heart.

Blessed John Francis Burté and Companions (I,III)
d. 1792 and 1794

These priests were victims of the French Revolution. Though their martyrdom spans a period of several years, they stand together in the Church's memory because they all gave their lives for the same principle. The Civil Constitution of the Clergy (1791) required all priests to take an oath which amounted to a denial of the faith. Each of these men refused and was executed.

John Francis Burté became a Franciscan at sixteen and after ordination taught theology to the young friars. Later he was guardian of the large Conventual friary in Paris until he was arrested and held in the convent of the Carmelites.

Appolinaris of Posat was born in 1739 in Switzerland. He joined the Capuchins and acquired a reputation as an excellent preacher, confessor and instructor of clerics. Sent to the East as a missionary, he was in Paris studying Oriental languages when the French Revolution began. Refusing the oath, he was swiftly arrested and detained in the Carmelite convent.

Severin Girault, a member of the Third Order Regular, was a chaplain for a group of sisters in Paris. Imprisoned with the others, he was the first to die in the slaughter at the convent.

These three plus 182 others — including several bishops and many religious and diocesan priests — were massacred at the Carmelite house in Paris on September 2, 1792. They were beatified in 1926.

John Baptist Triquerie, born in 1737, entered the Conventual Franciscans. He was chaplain and confessor of Poor Clare monasteries in three cities before he was arrested for refusing to take the oath. He and thirteen diocesan priests were guillotined in Laval on January 21, 1794. He was beatified in 1955.

Quote: "The upheaval which occurred in France toward the close of the eighteenth century wrought havoc in all things sacred and profane and vented its fury against the Church and her ministers. Unscrupulous men came to power who concealed their hatred for the Church under the deceptive guise of philosophy.... It seemed that the times of the early persecutions had returned. The Church, spotless bride of Christ, became resplendent with bright new crowns of martyrdom" (*Acts of Martyrdom*).

Comment: "Liberty, Equality, Fraternity" was the motto of the French Revolution. If individuals have "inalienable rights," as the Declaration of

Independence states, these must come not from the agreement of society (which can be very fragile) but directly from God. Do we believe that? Do we act on it?

Blessed Claudio Granzotto (I)
1900-1947

Born in Santa Lucia del Piave near Venice, Claudio was the youngest of nine children and was accustomed to hard work in the fields. At the age of nine he lost his father. Six years later he was drafted into the Italian army, where he served more than three years.

His artistic abilities, especially in sculpture, led to studies at Venice's Academy of Fine Arts, which awarded him a diploma with the highest marks in 1929. Even then he was especially interested in religious art. When Claudio entered the Friars Minor four years later, his parish priest wrote, "The Order is receiving not only an artist but a saint." Prayer, charity to the poor and artistic work characterized his life, which was cut short by a brain tumor. He died on the feast of the Assumption and was beatified in 1994.

Quote: In the beatification homily, Pope John Paul II said that Claudio made his sculpture "the privileged instrument" of his apostolate and evangelization. "His holiness was especially radiant in his acceptance of suffering and death in union with Christ's Cross. Thus by consecrating himself totally to the Lord's love, he became a model for religious, for artists in their search for God's beauty and for the sick in his loving devotion to the Crucified" (1994 LOR 47:1).

Comment: Claudio developed into such an excellent sculptor that his work still turns people toward God. No stranger to adversity, he met every obstacle courageously, reflecting the generosity, faith and joy that he learned from Francis of Assisi.

Saint Rose of Viterbo (III)
1233-1251

Rose achieved sainthood in only eighteen years of life. Even as a child Rose had a great desire to pray and to aid the poor. While still very young, she began a life of penance in her parents' house. She was as generous to the poor as she was strict with herself. At the age of ten she became a Secular Franciscan and soon began preaching in the streets about sin and the sufferings of Jesus.

Viterbo, her native city, was then in revolt against the pope. When Rose took the pope's side against the emperor, she and her family were exiled from the city. When the pope's side won in Viterbo, Rose was allowed to return. Her attempt at age fifteen to found a religious community failed, and she returned to a life of prayer and penance in her father's home, where she died in 1251. Rose was canonized in 1457.

Quote: Rose's dying words to her parents were: "I die with joy, for I desire to be united to my God. Live so as not to fear death. For those who live well in the world, death is not frightening, but sweet and precious."

Comment: The list of Franciscan saints seems to have quite a few men and women who accomplished nothing very extraordinary. Rose is one of them. She did not influence popes and kings, did not multiply bread for the hungry and never established the religious order of her dreams. But she made a place in her life for God's grace, and like Saint Francis before her, saw death as the gateway to new life.

Blessed Frederick Ozanam
1813-1853

A man convinced of the inestimable worth of each human being, Frederick served the poor of Paris well and drew others into serving the poor of the world. Through the St. Vincent de Paul Society, his work continues to the present day.

Frederick was the fifth of Jean and Marie Ozanam's fourteen children, one of only three to reach adulthood. As a teenager he began having doubts about his religion. Reading and prayer did not seem to help, but long walking discussions with Father Noirot of the Lyons College clarified matters a great deal.

Frederick wanted to study literature, although his father, a doctor, wanted him to become a lawyer. Frederick yielded to his father's wishes and in 1831 arrived in Paris to study law at the University of the Sorbonne. When certain professors there mocked Catholic teachings in their lectures, Frederick defended the Church.

A discussion club which Frederick organized sparked the turning point in his life. In this club Catholics, atheists and agnostics debated the issues of the day. Once, after Frederick spoke on Christianity's role in civilization, a club member said: "Let us be frank, Mr. Ozanam; let us also be very particular. What do you do besides talk to prove the faith you claim is in you?"

Frederick was stung by the question. He soon decided that his words needed a grounding in action. He and a friend began visiting Paris tenements and offering assistance as best they could. Soon a group dedicated to helping individuals in need under the patronage of Saint Vincent de Paul formed around Frederick.

Feeling that the Catholic faith needed an excellent speaker to explain its teachings, Frederick convinced the archbishop of Paris to appoint Father Lacordaire, the greatest preacher then in France, to preach a Lenten series in Notre Dame Cathedral. It was well attended and became an annual tradition in Paris.

After Frederick earned his law degree at the Sorbonne, he taught law at the University of Lyons. He also earned a doctorate in literature. Soon after marrying Amelie Soulacroix on June 23, 1841, he returned to the Sorbonne to teach literature. A well-respected lecturer, Frederick worked to bring out the best in each student. Meanwhile, the St. Vincent de Paul Society was growing throughout Europe. Paris alone counted twenty-five conferences.

In 1846, Frederick, Amelie and their daughter Marie went to Italy; there Frederick hoped to restore his poor health. They returned the next year. The revolution of 1848 left many Parisians in need of the services of the St. Vincent de Paul conferences. The unemployed numbered 275,000. The government asked Frederick and his coworkers to supervise the government aid to the poor. Vincentians throughout Europe came to the aid of Paris.

Frederick then started a newspaper, *The New Era*, dedicated to securing justice for the poor and the working classes. Fellow Catholics were often unhappy with what Frederick wrote. Referring to the poor man as "the nation's priest," Frederick said that the hunger and sweat of the poor formed a sacrifice that could redeem the people's humanity.

In 1852 poor health again forced Frederick to return to Italy with his wife and daughter. He died on September 8, 1853. In his sermon at Frederick's funeral, Lacordaire described his friend as "one of those privileged creatures who came direct from the hand of God in whom God joins tenderness to genius in order to enkindle the world."

Frederick was beatified in 1997. Since Frederick wrote an excellent book entitled *Franciscan Poets of the Thirteenth Century* and since Frederick's sense of the dignity of each poor person was so close to the thinking of Saint Francis, it seemed appropriate to include him in this book of Franciscan "greats."

Quote: Professor Bailly, the spirtual leader of the first St. Vincent de Paul conference, told Frederick and his first companions in charity, "Like Saint Vincent, you, too, will find the poor will do more for you than you will do for them."

Comment: "Those who mock the poor insult their Maker" (Proverbs 17:5). Frederick Ozanam never demeaned the poor in offering whatever service he could. Each man, woman and child was too precious for that. Serving the poor taught Frederick something about God that he could learn only there.

September 14

Pedro de Corpa and Companions (I)
d. 1597

These five friars were martyred in Georgia for their insistence on monogamy in Christian marriages.

In 1565 the Spanish established a fort and a settlement at St. Augustine, Florida. Pedro de Corpa came from Spain to Florida in 1587 and in the same year went to the missions among the Guale people in Georgia.

Pedro worked in Tolomato (near present Darien) where he converted a number of Guales and assisted their chief in running this Christian village. Juanillo, the chief's son, lapsed into polygamy and was urged to give this up. He refused and was publicly denounced and deprived of the right to succeed his father. Juanillo left, but only to gather some friends to help him seek vengeance on the friars. They killed Father Pedro several days later on September 13, 1597.

Father Blas de Rodriguez had come to Florida from Spain in 1580. He was the superior of the five martyred friars. Juanillo and his followers killed Blas on September 16 at the village of Tupiqui (near present Eulonia).

Father Miguel de Anon had come to Georgia in 1595; Brother Antonio de Badajoz in 1587. They were working together on St. Catherine's Island when Juanillo and his followers killed them on September 17.

Father Francisco de Berascola had come to Georgia in 1595 and founded the Misión Santo Domingo de Asao on St. Simon's Island. He was martyred by Juanillo's forces around September 18.

In 1605 the Guale missions were reestablished. They again began to prosper until English colonists arrived and destroyed all of them by 1702.

Quote: In 1612 the superior of the Custody of St. Helen (Florida and Cuba) reported to the king of Spain: "Although the Indians did not martyr the friars for the faith (that is, because of any doctrine or article of faith which they preached), it is certain that they martyred them because of the law of God which the religious taught them. This is the reason the Indians themselves gave and still attest to.... It is known in this land that, since the death of these holy religious, this people (the Guale Indians) has been docile and mild-mannered."

Comment: What would have happened if Pedro de Corpa and his companions had compromised Christ's teaching on monogamous marriage? They would have betrayed the very gospel they came to preach. Following Jesus always leads to hard choices — the cross — eventually.

Stigmata of Saint Francis

Francis lived out the Good News with such generosity and intensity that the stigmata, the marks of Christ's passion became imprinted on Francis' hands, feet and side.

Known for his poverty, in 1213 Francis accepted from Count Orlando of Chiusi the verbal gift of Mount La Verna, located between the Tiber and Arno rivers in the province of Arezzo, north of Rome. For ten years this mountain served Francis as a place of prayer and penance; it continues today as a place of pilgrimage and prayer.

Francis had such a great devotion to Saint Michael the Archangel that several times he observed a forty-day fast before the saint's feast on September 29. Near the feast of the Exaltation of the Holy Cross (September 14) in 1224, Francis had a vision of a six-winged angel, a seraph, and then realized that his hands, feet and side now bore the marks of Christ's passion.

The fact of the stigmata was known only to a few people in Francis' lifetime since he wanted to avoid any sensationalism about them or himself. Because these wounds caused him pain from time to time, Saint Clare made him a special pair of sandals to make walking easier. After his death in 1226, reliable witnesses, including the future popes Gregory IX and Alexander IV, testified that they had seen the stigmata on Francis' corpse. Many people eventually interpreted the stigmata as a recognition of Francis' radical conformity to Christ.

Pope Benedict XI (1303-04) allowed this feast to be observed within the Franciscan family.

Quote: "And because he [Francis] always bore and preserved Christ Jesus and him crucified in his heart with a wonderful love, he was marked in a most glorious way above all others with the seal of him whom in a rapture of mind he contemplated sitting in inexpressible and incomprehensible glory at the right hand of the Father, with whom he, the co-equal and most high Son of the Most High, lives and reigns, conquers and governs in union with the Holy Spirit, God eternally glorious through all ages forever. Amen" (2 *Celano*, #115).

Comment: Francis was quite ready to die as a martyr when he visited Egypt in 1220. God obviously wanted him to continue preaching the Good News and supporting that work with prayer as well as penance. The stigmata, which deepened Francis' humble service of God and neighbor, are a rare gift within God's people. Generously living out the Good News of Jesus should characterize all disciples.

Saint Joseph of Cupertino (I)
1603-1663

Joseph is most famous for levitating at prayer.

Already as a child, Joseph showed a fondness for prayer. After a short career with the Capuchins, he joined the Conventuals. Following a brief assignment caring for the friary mule, Joseph began his studies for the priesthood. Though studies were very difficult for him, Joseph gained a great deal of knowledge from prayer. He was ordained in 1628.

Joseph's tendency to levitate during prayer was sometimes a cross; some people came to see this much as they might have gone to a circus sideshow. Joseph's gift led him to be humble, patient and obedient, even though at times he was greatly tempted and felt forsaken by God. He fasted and wore iron chains for much of his life.

The friars transferred Joseph several times for his own good and for the good of the rest of the community. He was reported to and investigated by the Inquisition; the examiners exonerated him.

Joseph was canonized in 1767. In the investigation preceding the canonization, seventy incidents of levitation are recorded.

Quote: "Clearly, what God wants above all is our will which we received as a free gift from God in creation and possess as though our own. When a man trains himself to acts of virtue, it is with the help of grace from God from whom all good things come that he does this. The will is what man has as his unique possession" (Saint Joseph of Cupertino).

Comment: While levitation is an extraordinary sign of holiness, Joseph is also remembered for the ordinary signs he showed. He prayed even in times of inner darkness, and he lived out the Sermon on the Mount. He used his "unique possession" (his free will) to praise God and to serve God's creation.

Saint Francis Mary of Camporosso (I)
1804-1866

Saint Francis Mary gave himself generously to every task he was assigned by the friars.

Francis began his Franciscan life with the Capuchins in Genoa as a brother. Assigned to look after the sick friars, he fulfilled this service admirably. His next assignment, begging for the friary in Genoa, lasted forty years.

As the official beggar for the friars, he was well known to many people. He offered spiritual advice to adults and catechetical instructions to children. Part of his job was to share with the poor of Genoa the alms he collected each day. Eventually the people of that city referred to him as "the holy father."

Francis begged by day and spent a good many evenings praying before the Blessed Sacrament. When cholera broke out in Genoa, he gladly nursed its victims. He died of that disease. Francis Mary was canonized in 1962.

Quote: In the cemetery in Genoa, a statue of Saint Francis Mary bears the following inscription: "This poor man in Christ was more blessed in giving than in receiving. With bread and advice and consolation, he was ever prepared to minister to the sufferings and needs of all who came to him. His austere and holy life he crowned with the sacrifice he made of himself at the beginning of the epidemic of 1866. The sorrow and gratitude of the people prompted them to immortalize his image in this marble statue" (Marion A. Habig, O.F.M., *The Franciscan Book of Saints*, page 708).

Comment: Like it or not, holy men and women attract our attention. We admire their "faith working through love" (Galatians 5:6). Their self-sacrifice encourages us, just as the example of Francis Mary strengthened the people of Genoa.

Blessed Padre Pio of Piatrelcina (I)
1887-1968

Francesco Forgione's parents were farmers in Pietrelcina in southern Italy. Twice (1898-1903 and 1910-17) his father worked in Jamaica, New York, to provide the family income.

At the age of fifteen, Francesco joined the Capuchins and took the name of Pio. He was ordained in 1910 and was drafted during World War I. After he was discovered to have tuberculosis, he was discharged. In 1917 he was assigned to the friary in San Giovanni Rotondo, seventy-five miles from the city of Bari on the Adriatic.

On September 20, 1918, as he was making his thanksgiving after Mass, Padre Pio had a vision of Jesus. When the vision ended, he had the stigmata in his hands, feet and side.

Life became more complicated after that. Medical doctors, Church authorities and curiosity seekers came to see Padre Pio. In 1924 and again in 1931, the authenticity of the stigmata was questioned; Padre Pio was not permitted to celebrate Mass publicly or to hear confessions. He did not complain of these decisions, which were soon reversed. However, he wrote no letters after 1924. His only other writing, a pamphlet on the agony of Jesus, was done before 1924.

Padre Pio rarely left the friary after he received the stigmata, but busloads of people soon began coming to see him. Each morning after a 5 a.m. Mass in a crowded church, he heard confessions until noon. He took a mid-morning break to bless the sick and all who came to see him. Every afternoon he also heard confessions. In time his confessional ministry would take ten hours a day; penitents had to take a number so that the situation could be handled. Many of them have said that Padre Pio knew details of their lives that they had never mentioned.

Padre Pio saw Jesus in all the sick and suffering. At his urging, a fine hospital was built on nearby Mount Gargano. The idea arose in 1940; a committee began to collect money. Ground was broken in 1946. Building the hospital was a technical wonder because of the difficulty of getting water there and of hauling up the building supplies. This "House for the Alleviation of Suffering" has three hundred and fifty beds.

A number of people have reported cures they believe were received through the intercession of Padre Pio. Those who assisted at his Masses came away edified; several curiosity seekers were deeply moved. Like Saint Francis, Padre Pio sometimes had his habit torn or cut by souvenir hunters.

One of Padre Pio's sufferings was that unscrupulous people several times circulated prophecies that they claimed originated from him. He never made prophecies about world events and never gave an opinion on matters that he felt belonged to Church authorities to decide. He died on September 23, 1968, and was beatified in 1999.

Quote: Padre Pio once said, "The life of a Christian is nothing but a perpetual struggle against self; there is no flowering of the soul to the beauty of its perfection except at the price of pain."

Comment: Americans perhaps more than anyone else in the world today are interested in "how-to" books, magazines, newspaper columns and radio call-in shows. We are fascinated with technology and are constantly looking for shortcuts to save ourselves time and effort. But as Saint Francis and Padre Pio both knew, there is no shortcut in following the gospel, no way to avoid the "difficult teachings" of Jesus (see John 6:60). To preach a Christianity without personal sacrifice, without the cross, is no more authentic than the huckster who promises a patent medicine to cure all ills. Padre Pio was able to see his personal suffering as a response to his call to follow the gospel.

September 24

Saint Pacifico of San Severino (I)
1653-1721

Pacifico was born into a distinguished family in San Severino in the Marche of Ancona in central Italy. After joining the Friars Minor, he was ordained. He taught philosophy for two years and then began a successful preaching career.

Pacifico was an ascetic man. He fasted perpetually, eating no more than bread, soup or water. His "hair shirt" was made of iron. Poverty and obedience were two virtues for which his confreres especially remembered him.

At the age of thirty-five, Pacifico contracted an illness that eventually left him deaf, blind and crippled. He offered his sufferings for the conversion of sinners, and he cured many of the sick who came to him. Pacifico also served as the superior of the friary in San Severino. He was canonized in 1839.

Quote: "I also admonish and exhort these brothers that, in their preaching, their words be well chosen and chaste (cf. Ps 11:7; 17:31), for the instruction and edification of the people, speaking to them of vices and virtues, punishment and glory in a discourse that is brief, because it was in few words that the Lord preached while on earth" (Saint Francis, *Rule of 1223*, Chapter 9).

Comment: Pacifico lived out the words of Saint Francis cited above. His preaching and ministry were linked to his life of penance.

Francis urged his brothers to proclaim the Word of God without fanfare or self-interest. In that way, their words were truly God's and directed toward the welfare of their listeners. The way Pacifico lived made his preaching all the more effective, for his listeners knew the power present in his words.

September 26

Saint Elzear (III) and Blessed Delphina (III)
1286-1323; 1283-1358

This is the only Franciscan couple to be canonized or beatified formally. Elzear came from a noble family in southern France. After he married Delphina, she informed him that she had made a vow of perpetual virginity; that same night he did the same. For a time Elzear, Count of Ariano, was a counselor to Duke Charles of Calabria in southern Italy. Elzear ruled his own territories in the kingdom of Naples and in southern France with justice.

Elzear and Delphina joined the Secular Franciscans and dedicated themselves to the corporal works of mercy. Twelve poor people dined with them every day. A statue of Elzear shows him curing several people suffering from leprosy.

Their piety extended to the running of their household. Everyone there was expected to attend Mass daily, go to confession weekly and be ready to forgive injuries.

After Elzear's death, Delphina continued her works of charity for thirty-five more years. She is especially remembered for raising the moral level of the king of Sicily's court.

Elzear and Delphina are buried in Apt, France. He was canonized in 1369, and she was beatified in 1694.

Quote: Saint Bonaventure wrote: "Francis sought occasion to love God in everything. He delighted in all the works of God's hands and from the vision of joy on earth his mind soared aloft to the life-giving source and cause of all. In everything beautiful, he saw him who is beauty itself, and he followed his Beloved everywhere by his likeness imprinted on creation; of all creation he made a ladder by which he might mount up and embrace Him who is all-desirable" (*Legenda Major* IX:1).

Comment: Like Francis, Elzear and Delphina came to see all creation as pointing to its source. Therefore, they did not try ruthlessly to dominate any part of creation but used all of it as a way of returning thanks to God.

Though childless, their marriage was life-giving for the poor and the sick around them.

September 27

Mother Theresa Hackelmeier (III)
c. 1827-1860

A mere nine years after she arrived in the United States, Mother Theresa had established a community of Franciscan sisters which would grow to over six hundred members by the hundredth anniversary of her death.

Theresa Genevieve Hackelmeier was born in Europe around 1827. At the age of nine, she received her first Holy Communion and began a life-long devotion to the Eucharist. In her early teens she entered a convent in Vienna, Austria.

Nine years later at the invitation of Father Ambrose Buchmaier, a Franciscan missionary, she left that community and crossed the Atlantic to teach the children of German immigrants in Oldenburg, a small town in southeastern Indiana. When she arrived on January 6, 1851, Father Francis Joseph Rudolf, the pastor of Oldenburg, welcomed her and introduced her to three young women interested in forming a community of sisters. Within six years the group had grown to twenty-eight.

By 1852 the community staffed the town school and operated a girls' boarding school. The following year the sisters began perpetual adoration of the Blessed Sacrament. A year later they began to care for eleven orphans. Five other schools in the area were soon staffed by the sisters.

On January 23, 1857, the building housing the convent, orphanage and school burned to the ground. Mother Theresa barely escaped with her life. A woman of great hope in the face of this setback, she told her sisters: "Our good God has brought us together here; if this community is his work, he will help us, and we shall prosper; if it be the work of men, it will be dissolved."

Mother Theresa received permission from the bishops of Vincennes, Cincinnati and St. Louis to beg in their dioceses for funds to rebuild in Oldenburg. The begging tours were hard on her health, but she raised enough money to see the new convent completed. The sisters also petitioned several mission societies in Europe for funds to rebuild the convent and school.

At her death on September 27, 1860, the community numbered twenty-seven professed sisters, twelve novices and one postulant. Three sisters had already died. Today the Franciscan Sisters of Oldenburg, Indiana, are engaged in teaching, hospital work and pastoral ministry. They also work among the Crow Native Americans in Montana and the people of Papua, New Guinea.

Quote: On October 29, 1857, Mother Theresa wrote the members of the *Ludwig Missionsverein*, a Bavarian mission aid society, that work on the new convent and school had begun. She added, "How the money we receive will pay or defray the expenses of building God only knows." She closed the letter by saying, "Full of confidence that some day it will be our joy to greet you and to thank you, Reverend Sirs, in heaven as our benefactors, we are sending you our written petition in the holy name of Jesus."

Comment: Much of the personal information about Mother Theresa was destroyed in the 1857 fire, but she left her community the unforgettable example of a religious who, rather than give in to discouragement, conscientiously served the needs of her fellow sisters and who gave her best energies to the needs of the Church and the human family.

Saint John of Dukla (I)
1414-1484

Born in Dukla (Poland), John was a hermit briefly before entering the Conventuals in 1440. After his ordination his preaching ministry took him to what is now Ukraine, Moldavia and Belarus. He was local superior several times and once led the Franciscan custody headquartered in Lvív (Ukraine).

Saint John of Capistrano (October 23) came to Poland in 1453 and established friaries where the Rule of Saint Francis could be observed more strictly. Ten years later John of Dukla joined this Observant reform group, which later became the Province of the Immaculate Conception. Poverty, obedience, asceticism and devotion to Mary characterized John's life. He sought to reconcile schismatics to the Catholic Church. Although he became blind at age seventy, he still remained active as a preacher and confessor.

He was canonized at Krosno (Poland) in 1997 before approximately one million people who had come from Poland, Bohemia, Slovakia, Ukraine and Hungary.

Quote: At John of Dukla's canonization, Pope John Paul II said: "Jesus Christ was his only master. Imitating without reserve the example of his Master and Lord, he desired above all else to serve. In this consists the Gospel of wisdom, love and peace. He gave expression to this Gospel in the whole of his life" (1997 LOR 27:6).

Comment: In the canonization homily, Pope John Paul II recalled that the sons of Saint Francis arrived in Central Europe in the thirteenth century. "The Franciscan movement found fertile soil in our lands. It too bore fruit in a host of blesseds and saints who, following the example of the Poor Man of Assisi, enlivened Polish Christianity with the spirit of poverty and brotherly love. To the tradition of evangelical poverty and simplicity of life they added knowledge and wisdom, which in turn had an effect on their pastoral work."

Poverty, simplicity and the energetic search for truth have characterized the Franciscan approach to evangelization for almost eight centuries. They will enliven our witness to the Good News of Jesus Christ.

Saint Francis of Assisi
1182-1226

Francis' parents, Pica and Pietro, were part of Assisi's prosperous merchant class. A born leader, Francis instigated many revels among the young men of Assisi. Shaken by a year's imprisonment as a prisoner of war and by a long illness, Francis decided to abandon his knightly ambitions and dedicate himself to God's service. He would eventually describe himself as "the herald of the great king."

One day the crucifix at San Damiano, a dilapidated wayside chapel near Assisi, told him, "Rebuild my house, for it is nearly falling down." He then repaired San Damiano and two other nearby churches. That required begging stones in Assisi; Francis survived the occasional mocking that greeted him there.

Francis' life took a new direction when he met a man suffering from leprosy. Tempted to ride on, Francis dismounted, kissed the man and gave him some money. Later Francis and his followers would work among people suffering from leprosy. At the end of his life, Francis wrote of this incident on the road outside Assisi. "That which seemed bitter to me," he said, "was changed into sweetness of soul and body" (*Testament*). Francis overcame himself on that road and afterward was much more ready to care for the suffering.

Francis quickly attracted followers and in 1209 went to Rome to get approval from Pope Innocent III for this new group, originally called the "Penitents from Assisi." They dedicated themselves to prayer, manual labor and preaching the gospel. Their poverty lent credibility to their way of life.

By this time, however, many groups had formed to follow the gospel in poverty and simplicity. Some of these groups eventually separated themselves from the Church because, for one thing, they rejected the bishop's right to supervise preaching in his diocese. They also set themselves up as members of the "spiritual" (sinless) Church as opposed to the "carnal" (sinful) Church of their own day. Some of these groups also rejected the sacraments.

Francis wanted to show his loyalty to the Church from the very start. He succeeded in gaining verbal approval from the pope despite the doubts of some cardinals about whether such a radical following of Jesus was possible in the thirteenth century. In time Francis called his followers the Friars Minor (Lesser Brothers). As their numbers grew, he sent them throughout Europe. In 1219 he assigned Berard and his companions (January 16) to preach the gospel in Morocco. That same year Francis himself traveled to Egypt and the Holy Land.

When Francis returned to Assisi in 1220, he had become sick, and he realized that his group needed more capable administration than he could give it. Therefore he resigned as the leader. In the next two years, Francis devoted a lot of time to formulating a Rule to be submitted to the pope for approval. The final Rule was approved in 1223. Actually, Francis slipped in under the wire. The verbal approval given to his very small Rule of 1209 — a collection of Gospel texts — exempted him from the decision of the Fourth Lateran Council (1215) that no new religious Rules should be approved.

In response to Saint Clare's (August 11) desire to follow the gospel, Francis helped her organize the "Poor Ladies of San Damiano" (the Poor Clares). Lay men and women living "in the world" asked Francis to establish a group for them. The result was the Third Order — now known as the Secular Franciscan Order.

One of the best stories about Francis concerns "perfect joy." Francis once told Brother Leo, his secretary, to write that perfect joy would not be the news that all the masters of theology in Paris, all the bishops in Europe or the kings of France and England had joined the friars. Nor would perfect joy be the news that the friars had converted all non-Christians or that Francis had received the gift of miracles. No, perfect joy would be for Francis, worn out from travel, to come to the friars' lodging, identify himself, be refused entrance — and still keep his patience!

In September of 1224 while Francis was praying on Mount La Verna, he received the stigmata, the marks of Christ's passion on his hands, feet and side. Francis was able to hide this from many people, but he did attract a lot more attention from some people because of it. Growing blind and progressively weaker, in 1225 he composed his famous *Canticle of Brother Sun*. Francis died on the evening of October 3, 1226.

He was canonized in 1228 by his one-time advisor, the former Cardinal Hugolino and now Pope Gregory IX.

Quote: As Francis was dying, the bishop and the mayor of Assisi were at odds and had involved all of Assisi in the dispute. When both sides had assembled, Francis sent two friars to sing for them the *Canticle of Brother Sun*. Francis added the following verses especially for this occasion:

> Praised be You, my Lord, through those who give pardon for
>   Your love
> and bear infirmity and tribulation.

Blessed are those who endure in peace
for by You, Most High, they shall be crowned.

The bishop and the mayor settled their differences right then and there.

Comment: When the squeamish Francis kissed the man suffering from leprosy, a spiritual revolution was unleashed, for this act crowned Francis' conversion. How easy it would have been for Francis to cover his mouth and nose and throw the man a few coins! Francis overcame that reaction and so set the pattern for the rest of his life. He lived the gospel courageously, and he did so within the Church.

Francis rebuilt the Church by his example of prayer, penance and forgiveness. In owning nothing, he was eminently approachable and was well qualified to point out the path toward lasting peace.

October 6

Saint Mary Frances of the Five Wounds (III)
1715-1791

Anna Maria, a contemporary of the French Revolution, belonged to a middle-class family in Naples. When she was sixteen years old, a rich young man wanted to marry her. Her father agreed, but she insisted that she wanted to remain a virgin and to become a Franciscan tertiary. Her father whipped her and locked her in her room. He later agreed to allow her to become a tertiary and to be a consecrated virgin still living at home. She took the name Mary Frances.

Her father, brothers and sisters, however, did not always make life at home easy. Her confessor misunderstood her for a long time. Mary's life was absorbed in prayer, penance and the works of charity. She became the friend of the sick and needy of Naples; her penances gave her the resources to help the poor.

Mary, who was known for praying for the poor souls in purgatory, received the stigmata on her hands, feet and side. She was canonized in 1867.

Quote: "Charity unites us to God.... There is nothing mean in charity, nothing arrogant. Charity knows no schism, does not rebel, does all things in concord. In charity all the elect of God have been made perfect" (Saint Clement, *First Epistle to the Corinthians*, #49).

Comment: "Love is a decision," say the Marriage Encounter veterans. Charity is a costly virtue. It is never won once and for all. Over and over, Mary Frances had to face the same people and find a Christlike way of living with them. She is a saint because she kept making that decision to love.

October 10

Saint Daniel and Companions (I)
d. 1227

Inspired by the example of Saint Berard and his companions (January 16), seven Friars Minor led by Daniel, provincial of Calabria in southern Italy, went to preach the gospel in North Africa in 1227. They came to Ceuta, Morocco, where the Christian merchants warned them against preaching.

The friars, however, preached openly and were imprisoned for eight days. Bribes and then threats to make them renounce their faith were useless. Like the early Christian martyrs, they went to their deaths singing. Daniel and his companions were beheaded, and their bodies were taken to Spain. They were canonized in 1516.

Quote: "Martyrdom makes the disciples like their master, who willingly accepted death for the salvation of the world, and through it they are made like him by the shedding of blood. Therefore, the church considers it the highest gift and supreme test of love. And while it is given to few, all however must be prepared to confess Christ before humanity and to follow him along the way of the cross amid the persecutions which the church never lacks" (Vatican II, *Dogmatic Constitution on the Church*, #42).

Comment: Martyrs remind us of the high price Jesus paid for spreading the Good News. We are not free to choose the exact conditions of our witness to Jesus and the Good News. Remembering the martyrs of another era helps us persevere in living out the gospel that we, like Francis, are called to observe.

Blessed Mother Mary Angela Truszkowska (III)
1825-1899

A statue of Saint Felix of Cantalice (May 18) in the Capuchin church in Warsaw was a common stopping place for a new community of sisters instructing young children. Thus the people called these sisters Felicians.

Sophia, the eldest of seven, was born prematurely to Joseph and Josephine Truszkowska in Kalisz, Poland; she was not expected to live. At the age of fifteen, she went to Switzerland to convalesce from suspected tuberculosis. There she decided to redirect her life totally to God. She considered joining the Visitation sisters but decided instead to care for the most needy children of Warsaw. Sophia's cousin joined her in this work.

They entered the Third Order of Saint Francis under the direction of the Capuchins. In 1855 Sophia and Clothilde made a private consecration to the Blessed Mother. Two years later they and their companions received the Franciscan habit.

Their work among the homeless mushroomed, and their membership grew. Being a foundress was not easy for Sophia (now Mother Angela). Though some sisters wanted to follow a contemplative life, she felt this community was called by God to prayer and work outside the convent. The Felician sisters cared for the sick in their own homes; they also worked among the handicapped, aged, orphans and the homeless. The sisters established *ochrony* (shelters) for these people in Polish villages.

When the Poles revolted against the Russians in 1863, the sisters nursed the sick without regard to nationality. At this time Mother Angela wrote: "Among the sick, make no distinction; help them all without exception. Because of your vocation, you are obliged to exclude no one, for everybody is your neighbor" (Maria Winowska, Maria, *Go...Repair My House: Biography of Mother Mary Angela Truszkowska*, page 119).

In December of 1864 the Russian government disbanded the Felicians. Some of them regrouped with the Bernardine sisters in Lowicz. In 1865 the Austrian government allowed the sisters to reestablish themselves in the Austrian section of Poland.

When Mother Angela's health began to fail in 1869, she resigned her position as superior. Like Saint Francis before her, Mother Angela devoted her last years to prayer and manual labor. Tending the flowers in the convent garden was her service for some time. She also encouraged Sister Samuel's soup kitchen, which fed thousands of poor students at the University of Kraków.

On November 20, 1874, five Felician sisters arrived in Polonia, Wisconsin, in response to an invitation from Father Joseph Dabrowski (d. 1903) to teach the sons and daughters of Polish immigrants. The American mission eventually grew into seven provinces.

In her last years, Mother Angela prevailed upon Father Honoratus (December 16), the spiritual director of the community, to complete the constitutions of the new congregation. Shortly before Mother Angela died on October 10, 1899, the constitutions were approved in Rome.

The Felician sisters today number 3,600 members throughout the world. They work in education on all levels and also care for the sick, the homeless, orphans and the aged. Mother Angela was beatified in 1993.

Quote: Mother Angela once advised Sister Bogdana, "One 'Glory Be' said in adversity is worth more than a thousand thanksgivings in times of success."

Comment: Soon after Mother Angela died, one of her sisters described her as "an embodiment of the love of neighbor. For herself, only what was indispensable, strictly necessary — everything for others was her motto... not exposed as a banner, but realized by daily deeds over many years.... The pain of others, their anxieties, their suffering produced an echo in her heart, but it was not a fruitless echo. With admirable energy, despite her frail health, she sought remedial measures and almost always found them. This she did very naturally, as if that were her immediate obligation."

October 12

Saint Seraphin of Montegranaro (I)
1540-1604

Seraphin came from a poor Italian family where as a child he learned to love God. His childhood shepherd's job gave him plenty of time to pray. Refused admission by the Capuchins several times, he finally became a Capuchin brother in 1556. He had various jobs within the friary, and in all of them he edified the friars by his humility and generosity.

Seraphin imitated Saint Francis in fasting, clothing, courtesy to all and zeal for going to the missions. Permission for the latter, however, was not granted by Seraphin's superiors.

Three hours in prayer before the Blessed Sacrament were part of Seraphin's daily routine. The poor who begged at the friary door loved him. As the years went on, he felt a greater attraction to the contemplative life.

Seraphin died on October 12, 1604, and was canonized in 1767.

Quote: In *Brothers of Men*, Rene Voillaume of the Little Brothers of Jesus speaks about ordinary work and holiness: "Now this holiness [of Jesus] became a reality in the most ordinary circumstances of life, those of work, of the family and the social life of a village, and this is an emphatic affirmation of the fact that the most obscure and humdrum human activities are entirely compatible with the perfection of the Son of God." Christians are convinced, he says, "that the evangelical holiness proper to a child of God is possible in the ordinary circumstances of a man who is poor and obliged to work for his living" (pages 124-125).

Comment: For many people these days, work has no significance beyond providing the money they need to live. How many share the belief expressed in the Book of Genesis that we are to cooperate with God in caring for the earth? The kind of work Seraphin did may not strike us as earth-shattering. The work was ordinary: the spirit in which he did it was not.

October 22

Saint Peter of Alcantara (I)
1499-1562

Peter was a contemporary of Saint Paschal Baylon (May 17). Other sixteenth-century Spanish saints included John of the Cross, Ignatius of Loyola, Teresa of Avila, Francis Solano (July 14) and Salvator of Horta (March 18).

"Reform the Church" was the challenge in Peter's day. He directed all his energies to that end. Peter died the year before the Council of Trent ended.

Peter's parents were members of the nobility. After studying at the University of Salamanca, he joined the discalced (barefoot) Friars Minor in 1515. His abilities were soon recognized; he was named the superior of a new house even before his ordination (1524). At the age of thirty-nine, he was elected provincial; still he was not above washing dishes and cutting wood for the friars.

Peter was a successful preacher. He never gave in to the prejudices and passions of the day. The custom of erecting a special cross to commemorate the holding of a parish "mission" began with Peter.

Peter was penitential when it came to food and clothing. It is said that he slept only an hour and a half each night. He once observed that everyone talks about reform without trying to correct one's own heart. Peter's reform began with himself. His patience was so great that a proverb arose: "To bear such an insult one must have the patience of Peter of Alcantara."

In 1554, Peter received permission to form a group of friars who would follow the Rule of Saint Francis with even greater rigor. The friars who followed Peter's last reform were known as Alcantarines. Many of the Spanish friars who came to North and South America in the sixteenth, seventeenth and eighteenth centuries were members of this group. At the end of the nineteenth century, the Alcantarines were joined with other Observant friars to form the Order of Friars Minor.

Peter for some years offered spiritual direction to Saint Teresa of Avila and encouraged her in promoting the Carmelite reform. Peter's preaching brought many people to religious life, especially to the Secular Franciscan Order, the friars and the Poor Clares. Peter was canonized in 1669.

Quote: "I do not praise poverty for poverty's sake; I praise only that poverty which we patiently endure for the love of our crucified Redeemer and I consider this far more desirable than the poverty we undertake for the sake of poverty itself; for if I thought or believed otherwise, I would not seem to be firmly grounded in faith" (*Letter of Peter to Teresa of Avila*).

Comment: Poverty was a means and not an end for Peter. The goal was following Christ in ever greater purity of heart. Whatever obstructed that path could be eliminated with no real loss.

The philosophy of our consumer age — you are worth what you own — may find Peter of Alcantara's approach severe. Ultimately his approach is life-giving while consumerism is deadly.

Saint John of Capistrano (I)
1386-1456

John's period in history didn't lack excitement. The Great Western Schism, the Hundred Years' War and the fall of Constantinople all occurred in his lifetime.

John studied law at the University of Perugia and became a lawyer in Naples. Appointed governor of Perugia before he was thirty, John brought peace and justice to that region. As governor he was once thrown into prison during a civil war. There he reexamined his life and decided to become a Franciscan, which he did in 1416.

He and James of the Marche (November 28) studied theology under Bernardine of Siena (May 20). After his ordination in 1425, he began a successful preaching career in Italy. Large crowds heard him praise the beauty of God's ways and expose the ugliness of sin. So great was John's impact that cities petitioned the pope to send John to them. His nickname, "The Apostle of Europe," was well deserved.

Pope Eugene IV was especially grateful for John's wise advice. When the schismatic Council of Basel elected an anti-pope, John worked vigorously against popular support for that choice. The Church sent John to northern Italy to counter heretical groups there and he went to Bohemia to reconcile the Hussites.

John was a significant influence within the Order. Because of his preaching many young men joined the friars. By 1443 he held the highest post among the Observant friars in Italy. John declined the bishopric of Aquila and later of Rieti.

At the direction of Pope Callistus III, John preached a crusade to save western Europe from the Turks, who were advancing from recently conquered (1453) Constantinople, last outpost of the decimated Byzantine Empire. The Christians won a decisive victory at Belgrade in 1456.

Worn out from that crusade, John died on October 23, 1456. He was canonized in 1690.

Quote: John's tomb in Ilok, Croatia, bears this inscription: "This tomb holds John, by birth of Capistrano, a man worthy of all praise, defender and promoter of the faith, guardian of the Church, zealous protector of his Order, an ornament to all the world, lover of truth and justice, mirror of life, surest guide in doctrine; praised by countless tongues, he reigns blessed in heaven."

Comment: In John of Capistrano, Jesus found an energetic man. No hardship was too great, no self-sacrifice was too costly if John could show more people the wisdom of God's way and the folly of sin. John used his talents tirelessly for the spread of the gospel. Perhaps his example can help us to find energy we have not previously tapped.

Blessed Antônio de Sant'Anna Galvão (I)
1739-1822

God's plan in a person's life often takes unexpected turns which become life-giving through cooperation with God's grace.

Born in Guarantingueta near São Paulo (Brazil), Antônio attended the Jesuit seminary in Belem but later decided to become a friar. Invested in 1760, he made final profession the following year and was ordained in 1762.

In São Paulo, he served as preacher, confessor and porter. Within a few years he was appointed confessor to the Recollects of St. Teresa, a group of nuns in that city. He and Sister Helena Maria of the Holy Spirit founded a new community of sisters under the patronage of Our Lady of the Conception of Divine Providence. Sister Helena Maria's premature death the next year left Father Antônio responsible for the new congregation, especially for building a convent and church adequate for their growing numbers.

He served as novice master for the friars in Macacu and as guardian of St. Francis Friary in São Paulo. He founded St. Clare Friary in Sorocaba. With the permission of his provincial and the bishop, he spent his last days at the "Recolhimento de Nossa Senhora da Luz," the convent of the sisters' congregation he had helped establish.

He was beatified in Rome on October 25, 1998.

Quote: During the beatification homily, Pope John Paul II quoted from the Second Letter to Timothy (4:17), "The Lord stood by me and gave me strength to proclaim the word fully") and then said that Antônio "fulfilled his religious consecration by dedicating himself with love and devotion to the afflicted, the suffering and the slaves of his era in Brazil." The pope continued, "His authentically Franciscan faith, evangelically lived and apostolically spent in serving his neighbor, will be an encouragement to imitate this 'man of peace and charity.'"

Comment: Holy women and men cannot help calling our attention to God, to God's creation and to all the people whom God loves. The lives of holy people are so oriented toward God that this has become their definition of "normal." Do people see my life or yours as a living sign of God's steadfast love? What might have to change for that to happen?

November 3

Venerable Solanus Casey (I)
1870-1957

B arney Casey became one of Detroit's best-known priests even though he was not allowed to preach formally or to hear confessions!

Barney came from a large family in Oak Grove, Wisconsin. At the age of twenty-one, and after he had worked as a logger, a hospital orderly, a street car operator and a prison guard, he entered St. Francis Seminary in Milwaukee — where he found the studies difficult. He left there and, in 1896, joined the Capuchins in Detroit taking the name Solanus. His studies for the priesthood were again arduous.

On July 24, 1904, he was ordained, but because his knowledge of theology was judged to be weak, Father Solanus was not given permission to hear confessions or to preach. A Capuchin who knew him well said this annoying restriction "brought forth in him a greatness and a holiness that might never have been realized in any other way." During his fourteen years as porter and sacristan in Yonkers, New York, the people there recognized him as a fine speaker. "For, though he was forbidden to deliver doctrinal sermons," writes his biographer, James Derum, "he could give inspirational talks, or *feverinos*, as the Capuchins termed them" (18:96). His spiritual fire deeply impressed his listeners.

Father Solanus served at parishes in Manhattan and Harlem before returning to Detroit, where he was porter and sacristan for twenty years at St. Bonaventure Monastery. Every Wednesday afternoon he conducted well-attended services for the sick. A coworker estimates that on the average day 150 to 200 people came to see Father Solanus in the front office. Most of them came to receive his blessing; forty to fifty came for consultation. Many people considered him instrumental in cures and other blessings they received.

Father Solanus' sense of God's providence inspired many of his visitors. "Blessed be God in all his designs" was one of his favorite expressions.

The many friends of Father Solanus helped the Capuchins begin a soup kitchen during the Depression. Capuchins are still feeding the hungry there today.

In 1946 in failing health, he was transferred to the Capuchin novitiate in Huntington, Indiana, where he lived until 1956 when he was hospitalized in Detroit. He died on July 31, 1957. An estimated twenty thousand people passed by his coffin before his burial in St. Bonaventure Church in Detroit.

At the funeral Mass, Father Gerald, the provincial, said: "His was a life of service and love for people like me and you. When he was not himself sick, he nevertheless suffered with and for you that were sick. When he was not physically hungry, he hungered with people like you. He had a divine love for people. He loved people for what he could do for them — and for God, through them."

In 1960 a Father Solanus Guild was formed in Detroit to aid Capuchin seminarians. By 1967 the guild had five thousand members — many of them grateful recipients of his practical advice and his comforting assurance that God would not abandon them in their trials. He was declared Venerable in 1995.

Quote: Father Maurice Casey, a brother of Father Solanus, was once in a sanitarium near Baltimore and was annoyed at the priest-chaplain there. Father Solanus wrote his brother: "God could have established his Church under supervision of angels that have no faults or weaknesses. But who can doubt that as it stands today, consisting of and under the supervision of poor sinners—successors to the 'poor fishermen of Galilee' — the Church is a more outstanding miracle than any other way?"

Comment: James Patrick Derum, his biographer, writes that eventually Father Solanus was weary from bearing the burdens of the people who visited him. "Long since, he had come to know the Christ-taught truth that pure love of God and one's fellowmen as children of God are in the final event all that matter. Living this truth ardently and continuously had made him, spiritually, a free man — free from slavery to passions, from self-seeking, from self-indulgence, from self-pity — free to serve wholly both God and man" (*The Porter of St. Bonaventure's*, page 199).

Saint Charles Borromeo (III)
1538-1584

Catholics who feel Vatican II set in motion tremendous changes in the Church may feel some sympathy for the Catholics in Charles Borromeo's day. Both Vatican II and the Council of Trent, with which Charles Borromeo was closely connected, set in motion far-reaching changes in the Church. The Council of Trent was held piecemeal between 1545 and 1563. After its conclusion, the main responsibility for enacting new reforms fell on bishops like Charles Borromeo.

Charles was born into a prominent family. His mother was a Medici and Pope Pius IV was his uncle. After receiving doctorates in canon and civil law from the University of Pavia, Charles was appointed the pope's Secretary of State. In that capacity Charles could easily have turned out to be a self-indulgent officeholder. Instead, he gave his best energies to the job and helped complete the Council of Trent.

At the age of twenty-five, he was appointed archbishop of Milan. His first priority was to implement the reforms called for by the council. He was especially well known for establishing the Confraternity of Christian Doctrine throughout his archdiocese.

Not everyone was happy with Bishop Borromeo; he survived an assassination attempt. Interested in social problems, Charles did not let his position prevent him from ministering to the victims of the epidemic that swept through Milan in 1676. He even sold some of his possessions to raise money to help them.

Charles Borromeo became a Secular Franciscan early in life and later served as Cardinal Protector of the Franciscans. These factors probably influenced his love for simplicity and his penitential spirit. Charles died at the age of forty-six; he was canonized in 1610.

Quote: "I admonish and exhort the brothers in the Lord Jesus Christ that they beware of all pride, vainglory, envy, avarice (cf. Lk 12:15), cares and worries of this world (cf. Mt 13:22), detraction and complaint" (Saint Francis, *Rule of 1223*, Chapter 10).

Comment: Francis' advice to the friars summarizes the generous service Charles Borromeo offered to Christ's Church. Proud, envious and greedy people consume much of their energy worrying about themselves. Charles simplified his life so that he would have the time and energy to care for God's people as best he could. Is the gospel calling us to simplify our lives even more?

Saint Didacus of Alcalá (I)
1400-1463

Didacus is living proof that God "chose what is foolish in the world to shame the wise; God chose what is weak in the world to shame the strong" (1 Corinthians 1:27).

As a young man in Spain, Didacus joined the Secular Franciscan Order and lived for some time as a hermit. After Didacus became a Franciscan brother, he developed a reputation for great insight into God's ways. His penances were heroic. Didacus was so generous with the poor that the friars sometimes grew uneasy about his charity.

Didacus volunteered for the missions in the Canary Islands and labored there energetically and profitably. He was also the superior of a friary there.

In 1450 he was sent to Rome to attend the canonization of Saint Bernardine of Siena (May 20). When many friars gathered for that celebration fell sick, Didacus stayed in Rome for three months to nurse them. After he returned to Spain, he pursued a life of contemplation full time. He showed the friars the wisdom of God's ways.

As he was dying, Didacus looked at a crucifix and said: "O faithful wood, O precious nails! You have borne an exceedingly sweet burden, for you have been judged worthy to bear the Lord and King of heaven" (Marion A. Habig, O.F.M., *The Franciscan Book of Saints*, page 834).

San Diego, California, is named for this Franciscan, who was canonized in 1588.

Quote: "He was born in Spain with no outstanding reputation for learning, but like our first teachers and leaders unlettered as men count wisdom, an unschooled person, a humble lay brother in religious life. [God chose Didacus] to show in him the abundant riches of his grace to lead many on the way of salvation by the holiness of his life and by his example and to prove over and over to a weary old world almost decrepit with age that God's folly is wiser than men, and his weakness is more powerful than men" (*Bull of Canonization*).

Comment: We cannot be neutral about genuinely holy people. We either admire them or we consider them foolish. Didacus is a saint because he used his life to serve God and God's people. Can we say the same for ourselves?

Blessed John Duns Scotus (I)
1266-1308

A humble man, John Duns Scotus has been one of the most influential Franciscans through the centuries.

Born at Duns in the county of Berwick, Scotland, John was descended from a wealthy farming family. In later years he was identified as John Duns Scotus to indicate the land of his birth; *Scotia* is the Latin name for Scotland.

John received the habit of the Friars Minor at Dumfries, where his uncle Elias Duns was superior. After novitiate John studied at Oxford and Paris and was ordained in 1291. More studies in Paris followed until 1297, when he returned to lecture at Oxford and Cambridge. Four years later he returned to Paris to teach and complete the requirements for the doctorate.

In an age when many people adopted whole systems of thought without qualification, John pointed out the richness of the Augustinian-Franciscan tradition, appreciated the wisdom of Aquinas, Aristotle and the Muslim philosophers — and still managed to be an independent thinker. That quality was proven in 1303 when King Philip the Fair tried to enlist the University of Paris on his side in a dispute with Pope Boniface VIII. John Duns Scotus dissented and was given three days to leave France.

In Scotus's time, some philosophers held that people are basically determined by forces outside themselves. Free will is an illusion, they argued. An ever practical man, Scotus said that if he started beating someone who denied free will, the person would immediately tell him to stop. But if Scotus didn't really have a free will, how could he stop? John had a knack for finding illustrations his students could remember!

After a short stay in Oxford, he returned to Paris, where he received the doctorate in 1305. He continued teaching there and in 1307 so ably defended the Immaculate Conception of Mary that the university officially adopted his position. That same year the minister general assigned him to the Franciscan school in Cologne where John died in 1308. He is buried in the Franciscan church near the famous Cologne cathedral.

Drawing on the work of John Duns Scotus, Pope Pius IX solemnly defined the Immaculate Conception of Mary in 1854. John Duns Scotus, the "Subtle Doctor," was beatified in 1993.

Quote: Father Charles Balic, O.F.M., the foremost twentieth-century authority on Scotus, wrote: "The whole of Scotus's theology is dominated by the notion of love. The characteristic note of this love is its absolute freedom. As love becomes more perfect and intense, freedom becomes more noble and integral both in God and in man" (*New Catholic Encyclopedia*, volume 4, page 1105).

Comment: Intelligence hardly guarantees holiness. But John Duns Scotus was not only brilliant, he was also humble and prayerful — the exact combination Saint Francis wanted in any friar who studied. In a day when French nationalism threatened the rights of the pope, Scotus sided with the papacy and paid the price. He also defended human freedom against those who would compromise it by determinism.

Ideas are important. John Duns Scotus placed his best thinking at the service of the human family and of the Church.

November 14

Saint Nicholas Tavelić and Companions (I)
d. 1391

Nicholas and his three companions are among the 158 Franciscans who have been martyred in the Holy Land since the friars became custodians of the shrines in 1335.

Nicholas was born in 1340 to a wealthy and noble family in Croatia. He joined the Franciscans and was sent with Deodat of Rodez to preach in Bosnia. In 1384 they volunteered for the Holy Land missions and were sent there. They looked after the holy places, cared for the Christian pilgrims and studied Arabic.

In 1391 Nicholas, Deodat, Peter of Narbonne and Stephen of Cuneo decided to take a direct approach to converting the Muslims. On November 11, 1391, they went to the huge Mosque of Omar in Jerusalem and asked to see the Qadi (Muslim official). Reading from a prepared statement, they said that all people must accept the gospel of Jesus. When they were ordered to retract their statement, they refused. After beatings and imprisonment, they were beheaded before a large crowd.

Nicholas and his companions were canonized in 1970. They are the only Franciscans martyred in the Holy Land to be canonized.

Quote: In the *Rule of 1221*, Francis wrote that the friars who go to the Saracens and nonbelievers "can live spiritually in two ways. One way is not to engage in arguments or disputes, but to be subject to every human creature for God's sake (1 Pet 2:13) and to acknowledge that they are Christians. Another way is to proclaim the word of God when they see that it pleases the Lord, so that they believe in the all-powerful God — Father, and Son, and Holy Spirit — the Creator of all, in the Son Who is the Redeemer and Savior, and that they be baptized and become Christians" (Chapter 16).

Comment: Francis presented two missionary approaches for his friars. Nicholas and his companions followed the first approach (live quietly and give witness to Christ) for several years. Then they felt called to take the second approach of preaching openly. Their Franciscan confreres in the Holy Land are still working by example to make Jesus better known.

November 15

Mary of the Passion (III)
1839-1904

O ver the years Mary grew to understand how she could best serve God. Born Helene de Chappotin de Neuville, she came from a distinguished French family in Nantes. In 1860 she entered the Poor Clares, but poor health forced her to leave the following year. In 1864 she joined the Sisters of Mary Reparatrix and took the name Mary of the Passion. From 1865 to 1876 she worked in the Madura missions in India. In 1877 she established the Institute of the Missionaries of Mary, which became the Franciscan Missionaries of Mary (F.M.M.) in 1882 when she adopted the Third Order Rule.

Mary was still living when seven members of her community were martyred in the 1900 Boxer Uprising (see July 8 martyrs). In addition to caring for people afflicted with leprosy, her sisters have served in education, social service, nursing and catechetics—frequently with F.M.M.'s of other nationalities.

Her cause for beatification has been introduced in Rome.

Quote: Mary once said, "I wish I had two lives: one with which I could always pray, the other, with which to perform all the duties God imposes on me."

Comment: Exactly what duties did God impose on Mary? Did he reveal to her precisely what work her sisters were to do? In prayer, Mary's heart was purified, and she conformed even more to God's ways. Prayer certainly led her to see ways of serving that she had not previously realized.

November 16

Pamfilo da Magliano (I)

1824-1876

Spreading the gospel of Jesus Christ recognizes no national boundaries. This Italian friar volunteered to teach Irish Franciscans and eventually was sent to look after German and Irish immigrants in southwest New York.

John Paul Pierbattista was born in Magliano dei Marsi and entered the Franciscans when he was sixteen. Receiving the name Pamfilo, he made his profession, completed his studies and was ordained in 1846.

For the next six years he taught philosophy and theology in his province (Abruzzi). When the Irish Franciscans asked for a friar to teach theology at their college in Rome (St. Isidore's), Father Pamfilo was sent. Three years later he volunteered to work among the Irish and German immigrants in the Diocese of Buffalo.

Nicholas Devereux of Utica, New York, had promised cash and land if the Franciscans would come to Allegany in southwestern New York. Bishop Timon of Buffalo heartily approved of Devereux's offer and pursued this request with the Franciscan minister general. Father Pamfilo was appointed superior of the group, which included two other priests and a brother. They arrived in New York City on June 20, 1855.

In the twelve years that Father Pamfilo worked in the United States, he was responsible for establishing five parishes and twenty-two mission churches. In 1858 the building destined to serve as college, seminary, secondary school and residence for the friars was completed in Allegany. In September of the following year, the Franciscan college — now St. Bonaventure University — was established. Father Pamfilo founded and directed Christ the King Seminary which was on the grounds of the university for many years and has now been relocated to East Aurora, New York.

In 1859 Father Pamfilo invested Mother Teresa O'Neil (May 12) and two other young women, the first members of a community of Franciscan sisters in Allegany. Staffing the two academies for young women in the area was their first work. By 1862 the community had three professed members and five novices. He was also instrumental in establishing the community of Franciscan sisters in Joliet, Illinois, in 1865.

In addition to his other responsibilities, Father Pamfilo served as superior of the newly formed Custody of the Immaculate Conception. Friars of that custody soon served in parishes in Connecticut, Massachusetts, Pennsylvania and Texas. Rumors of misadministration prompted his recall to Rome where he was vindicated of any wrongdoing. His wish to be relieved of his job as superior and to remain in Italy was granted.

In 1867 he published a life of Saint Francis. In the remaining years of his life, Father Pamfilo published two volumes of his history of the Franciscan Order. The third volume of his history of the Order was hardly begun at his death on November 15, 1876.

Quote: Father Hyacinth Marinangeli, O.F.M., writes: "All those who have interested themselves in the life and work of Father Pamfilo...have agreed on emphasizing his vast learning, his sure and modern didactics, his prodigious industry, his singular capacity to organize and to accomplish much, his childlikeness and altruism to the point of heroism, and his profound piety. He was a true son of St. Francis and a genuine 'man of God,' in the all-encompassing, simple expression of one of the first pupils of St. Bonaventure, and a citizen who made illustrious the land of his birth, a man of religion who honored his Order and the Church, a rigorous scholar who contributed to knowledge of the Franciscan movement and to the history of the Order particularly in Italy" ("The Dynamic Missionary Life of Father Pamfilo da Magliano," *Abrouzzosette*, November 11, 1976).

Comment: Like Saint Paul before him, Father Pamfilo planted the seed that others would nourish. In time his schools, communities of friars and congregations of Franciscan women would grow strong and bear a striking witness to the Good News of Jesus.

Saint Elizabeth of Hungary
Patroness of the Secular Franciscan Order
1207-1231

E lizabeth can teach us to work against injustice without becoming warped by bitterness.

Elizabeth did so much that it is hard to believe she was only twenty-four at her death. Her father was King Andrew II of Hungary. At the age of three, she went to Thuringia (eastern Germany) to be raised in the court of her future husband, Louis. As a child she developed strong habits of prayer and the works of charity. As a princess she used to remove her crown on entering a church, saying she could not bear to be richly crowned where Christ was wearing a crown of thorns.

Louis and Elizabeth had four children. She cared for them well and continued her charity, building a large hospital at Eisenach and feeding the hungry. Elizabeth did not leave the corporal works of mercy to others; she served food and dressed wounds. A member of the Secular Franciscan Order, she shared Francis' compassion for those afflicted with leprosy.

The most famous story about Elizabeth concerns her generosity, which Louis sometimes criticized. One December day while carrying bread to the poor, she unexpectedly met him. After Louis demanded to see what she was carrying, she unrolled her cloak and revealed fresh roses. He made no further objection.

Elizabeth's generosity to the poor provoked a certain amount of jealousy at the court. In 1227, Louis joined Emperor Frederick II's crusade to the Holy Land. After Louis's death in southern Italy, his mother and brother drove Elizabeth and her four children from the castle in mid-winter.

She was eventually restored to her rightful position. After providing for the education of her children, she retired to Marburg where she nursed the sick.

Elizabeth was canonized four years after her death; she is the patroness of the Secular Franciscan Order and of Catholic Charities.

Quote: What Pope Paul VI once said of Mother Teresa of Calcutta is equally true of Elizabeth of Hungary: "We discover a law: that good multiplies itself. The work of Mother Teresa shows this. Her inexhaustible energy, her potential for good, the resource of her human heart, are poured out. The leaven of her personal sacrifice as well as her courage made her do unbelievable things with God's help" (quoted in Boniface Hanley, O.F.M., *Ten Christians*, page 125).

Comment: What kept Elizabeth from becoming bitter and vindictive when driven from her palace and her position as regent for the absent king? By that time she had cooperated with God's grace so generously that his standards had become an essential part of her life.

Elizabeth also shows us a personal way of serving the suffering Christ in his various "distressing disguises."

November 19

Saint Agnes of Assisi (II)
1197-1253

Agnes was the sister of Clare (August 11) and her first follower. When Agnes left home two weeks after Clare's departure, their family attempted to bring Agnes back by force. They tried to drag her out of the monastery, but all of a sudden her body became so heavy that several knights could not budge it. Her uncle Monaldo tried to strike her but was temporarily paralyzed. The knights then left Agnes and Clare in peace.

Agnes matched her sister in devotion to prayer and in willingness to endure the strict penances which characterized their lives at San Damiano. In 1221 a group of Benedictine nuns in Monticelli (near Florence) asked to become Poor Clares. Saint Francis sent Agnes to become abbess of that monastery. Agnes soon wrote a rather sad letter about how much she missed Clare and the other nuns at San Damiano. After establishing other Poor Clare monasteries in northern Italy, Agnes was recalled to San Damiano in 1253 when Clare was dying.

Agnes followed Clare in death three months later. Agnes was canonized in 1753.

Quote: Charles de Foucald, founder of the Little Brothers and Sisters of Jesus, said: "One must pass through solitude and dwell in it to receive God's grace. It is there that one empties oneself, that one drives before oneself all that is not God, and that one completely empties this little house of our soul to leave room for God alone. In doing this, do not fear being unfaithful toward creatures. On the contrary, that is the only way for you to serve them effectively" (Raphael Brown, *Franciscan Mystic*, page 126).

Comment: God must love irony; the world is so full of it. In 1212, many in Assisi surely felt that Clare and Agnes were wasting their lives and were turning their backs on the world. In reality, their lives were tremendously life-giving, and the world has been enriched by the example of these poor contemplatives.

Margaret Sinclair (II)
1900-1925

Margaret was born in Edinburgh, Scotland, where her father worked for the department of sanitation. The Sinclair family (three girls, three boys) lived in "Auld Reekie," the Irish sector of Edinburgh. Their faith was nourished at St. Patrick's Parish.

As a child Margaret was a determined athlete and an excellent student. After finishing grammar school, she worked in a furniture factory and studied home economics in night school. World War I saw her father and brother called into service. Margaret and the rest of the family took up gardening in government-provided land to supplement the family food supply.

When World War I ended, she worked as a clerk at the McVitie Biscuit Shop, where she was well liked by her employer and coworkers. Already a daily communicant for some years, Margaret began spending more time before the Blessed Sacrament in these years. Generosity to the poor also became a bigger part of her life.

In 1923, Margaret entered the Poor Clare monastery in Notting Hill, England, as an extern sister — one who does the errands and takes care of the door so that the other sisters may pursue a life of contemplation. Her name as a Poor Clare was Sister Mary Francis of the Five Wounds.

In February of 1925, tuberculosis was diagnosed and she was sent to the sanitarium of the Sisters of Charity in Warley. Having borne her pains bravely, she died on November 24 of that year.

Quote: Before her profession, Sister Mary Francis wrote in her journal, "O my God, help me always to take up thy cross and cheerfully to follow thee."

Comment: The cross of Jesus rarely comes to us from the direction we had expected it. When Margaret wrote the words cited above, she did not know what the future would be. But what did that matter? Whatever happened, God would be with her. People assured of that are always a great source of strength to others.

November 26

Saint Leonard of Port Maurice (I)
1676-1751

Leonard, called "the great missionary of the eighteenth century" by Saint Alphonsus Ligouri, was another Franciscan who tried to go to the foreign missions (China), failed at that and succeeded tremendously in some other work.

Leonard's father was a ship captain whose family lived in Port Maurice on the northwestern coast of Italy. At thirteen, Leonard went to Rome to live with his uncle Agostino and study at the Roman College. Leonard was a good student and was destined for a career in medicine. In 1697, however, he joined the Friars Minor, a decision that his uncle opposed bitterly.

After ordination Leonard contracted tuberculosis and was sent to his hometown to rest or perhaps to die. He made a vow that if he recovered he would dedicate his life to the missions and to the conversion of sinners. He soon was able to begin his forty-year career of preaching retreats, Lenten sermons and parish missions throughout Italy. His missions lasted fifteen to eighteen days, and he often stayed an additional week to hear confessions. He said: "I believe that in those days the real and greatest fruit of the mission is gathered. As much good is done in these days as during the mission."

As a means of keeping alive the religious fervor awakened in a mission, Leonard promoted the Stations of the Cross, a devotion which had made little progress in Italy up to this time. He also preached regularly on the Holy Name of Jesus.

Since he realized that he needed time simply to pray alone, Leonard regularly made use of the *ritiros* (houses of recollection) that he helped establish throughout Italy.

Leonard was canonized in 1867; in 1923 he was named patron of those who preach parish missions.

Quote: Saint Leonard once said, "If the Lord at the moment of my death reproves me for being too kind to sinners, I will answer, 'My dear Jesus, if it is a fault to be too kind to sinners, it is a fault I learned from you, for you never scolded anyone who came to you seeking mercy'" (Leonard Foley, O.F.M., "St. Leonard of Port Maurice," page 9).

Comment: The success of someone who comes in and conducts a retreat or leads a city-wide "crusade" depends on whether the fervor generated can be sustained over the long run. Changed lives make the difference. For Leonard, the Stations of the Cross and regular confession helped people maintain the personal reforms initiated during his preaching. When was the last time you prayed the Stations of the Cross?

November 27

Saint Francesco Antonio Fasani (I)
1681-1742

Born in Lucera (southeast Italy), Francesco entered the Conventuals in 1695. After his ordination ten years later, he taught philosophy to younger friars, served as guardian of his friary and later became provincial. When his term of office ended, Francesco became master of novices and finally pastor in his hometown.

In his various ministries, he was loving, devout and penitential. He was a sought-after confessor and preacher. One witness at the canonical hearings regarding Francesco's holiness testified, "In his preaching he spoke in a familiar way, filled as he was with the love of God and neighbor; fired by the Spirit, he made use of the words and deed of Holy Scripture, stirring his listeners and moving them to do penance." Francesco showed himself a loyal friend of the poor, never hesitating to seek from benefactors what was needed.

At his death in Lucera, children ran through the streets and cried out, "The saint is dead! The saint is dead!" Francesco was canonized in 1986.

Quote: During his homily at the canonization of Francesco, Pope John Paul II reflected on John 21:15 in which Jesus asks Peter if he loves Jesus more than the other apostles and then tells Peter, "Feed my lambs." The pope observed that in the final analysis human holiness is decided by love. "He [Francesco] made the love taught us by Christ the fundamental characteristic of his existence, the basic criterion of his thought and activity, the supreme summit of his aspirations" (1986 LOR 16:3).

Comment: Eventually we become what we choose. If we choose stinginess, we become stingy. If we choose compassion, we become compassionate. The holiness of Francesco Antonio Fasani resulted from his many small decisions to cooperate with God's grace.

November 28

Saint James of the Marche (I)
1394-1476

Meet one of the fathers of the modern pawnshop!

James was born in the Marche of Ancona, in central Italy along the Adriatic Sea. After earning doctorates in canon and civil law at the University of Perugia, he joined the Friars Minor and began a very austere life. He fasted nine months of the year; he slept three hours a night. Saint Bernardine of Siena (May 20) told him to moderate his penances.

James studied theology with Saint John of Capistrano (October 23). Ordained in 1420, James began a preaching career that took him all over Italy and through thirteen Central and Eastern European countries. This extremely popular preacher converted many people (250,000 at one estimate) and helped spread devotion to the Holy Name of Jesus. His sermons prompted numerous Catholics to reform their lives and many men joined the Franciscans under his influence.

With John of Capistrano, Albert of Sarteano and Bernardine of Siena, James is considered one of the "four pillars" of the Observant movement among the Franciscans. These friars became known especially for their preaching.

To combat extremely high interest rates, James established *montes pietatis* (literally, mountains of charity) — nonprofit credit organizations that lent money at very low rates on pawned objects.

Not everyone was happy with the work James did. Twice assassins lost their nerve when they came face to face with him. James was canonized in 1726.

Quote: "Beloved and most holy word of God! You enlighten the hearts of the faithful, you satisfy the hungry, console the afflicted; you make the souls of all productive of good and cause all virtues to blossom; you snatch souls from the devil's jaw; you make the wretched holy, and men of earth citizens of heaven" (*Sermon of St. James*).

Comment: James wanted the word of God to take root in the hearts of his listeners. His preaching was directed to preparing the soil, so to speak, by removing any rocks and softening up lives hardened by sin. God's intention is that his word take root in our lives, but for that we need both prayerful preachers and cooperative listeners.

November 29

All the Saints of the Seraphic Order

Just as the Church observes November 1 as the Feast of All Saints, so the Franciscans on this day remember all the men and women of all three Orders who are with God. Obscurity does not lessen the holiness of any man or woman.

Who are the people most influential in your Franciscan vocation? This is a day to remember the holiness of those men and women. Who were the first Franciscans to preach in your corner of the world? Today you can thank God for their zeal and example. In one list of saints and blesseds of the three Orders, over half the entries were missionary martyrs.

Quote: "I speak to you, my son, as a mother. I place all the words which we spoke on the road in this phrase, briefly and [as] advice. And afterwards, if it is necessary for you to come to me for counsel, I say this to you: In whatever way it seems best to you to please the Lord God and to follow His footprints and His poverty, do this with the blessing of God and my obedience" (Saint Francis, *Letter to Brother Leo*).

Comment: Truly the saints of all three Orders are the "very great multitude" predicted by Saint Francis (*1 Celano*, #27). They are not an excuse for boasting but rather are a challenge to the generosity of our faith.

In an age that seems gradually to be recognizing a "right to die" according to one's own preference, these Franciscan saints remind us of our ability to choose how we will live now.

John of Monte Corvino (I)
1247-1328

At a time when the Church was heavily embroiled in nationalistic rivalries within Europe, it was also reaching across Asia to spread the gospel of Jesus Christ to the Mongols. John of Monte Corvino went to China about the same time Marco Polo was returning.

John was a soldier, judge and doctor before he became a friar. Prior to going to Tabriz, Persia (present-day Iran) in 1278, he was well-known for his preaching and teaching. In 1291 he left Tabriz as a legate of Pope Nicholas IV to the court of Kublai Khan. John, an Italian merchant and a Dominican friar traveled to western India, where the Dominican died. When John and the Italian merchant arrived in China in 1294, Kublai Khan had recently died.

Nestorian Christians, successors to the dissidents of the fifth-century Council of Ephesus' teaching on Jesus Christ, had been in China since the seventh century. John converted some of them and also some of the Chinese, including Prince George from Tenduk, northwest of Beijing. Prince George named his son after this holy friar.

John established his headquarters in Khanbalik (now Beijing), where he built two churches; his was the first resident Catholic mission in the country. By 1304 he had translated the Psalms and the New Testament into the Tatar language.

Responding to two letters from John, Pope Clement V named John Archbishop of Khanbalik in 1307 and consecrated seven friars as bishops of neighboring dioceses. One of the seven never left Europe. Three others died along the way to China; the remaining three bishops and the friars who accompanied them arrived there in 1308.

When John died in 1328, he was mourned by Christians and non-Christians. His tomb quickly became a place of pilgrimage. In 1368, Christianity was banished from China when the Mongols were expelled and the Ming dynasty began. John's cause has been introduced in Rome.

Quote: In 1975, Pope Paul VI wrote, "The Church evangelizes when she seeks to convert, solely through the divine power of the Message she proclaims, both the personal and collective consciences of people, the activities in which they engage, and the lives and concrete milieus which are theirs" (*Evangelization in the Modern World*, #18).

Comment: When John of Monte Corvino went to China, he represented the Church's desire to preach the gospel to a new culture and to be enriched by it. The travels of Pope John Paul II have demonstrated the universality of the Good News and the urgent need to continue the challenging work of helping the Good News take root in a variety of cultural situations.

December 1

Rembert Kowalski (I)
1884-1970

A young Polish man who joined a largely German province spent most of his life either working in China or praying for the conversion of the Chinese people.

Rembert's parents came from Poland to the United States in 1882; his father worked at a copper mine in Calumet, Michigan. In 1898 Rembert went to the Franciscan seminary in Cincinnati. The day before he was to be ordained in 1911, his father was killed in a mining accident.

Sent to Gallup, New Mexico, to care for the Slavic miners nearby, the young priest worked there until 1925 when he was transferred to Peña Blanca, New Mexico. In December of that year, a letter to all the friars of St. John the Baptist Province invited them to volunteer for the Chinese missions. Rembert was the only friar to volunteer at the first invitation. The following August he and three newly ordained priests sailed for China.

Their destination, Wuchang in the province of Hubei, was then under the control of the Chinese communists; Sylvester Espelage of St. John the Baptist Province was prefect apostolic in that city. When Father Kowalski finally arrived in Wuchang, he was assigned to a nearby mission and then put in charge of the local minor seminary. Assignments as hospital chaplain and superior of the friars followed.

In 1937 the Japanese-Chinese War began; Wuchang was occupied by the Japanese until the end of World War II. In January, 1942, Rembert was consecrated bishop; the following year he started a thirty-month imprisonment under the Japanese. When the war ended, the bishop began rebuilding his vicariate, which became a diocese in 1946. Five years later he was imprisoned by the communists. After 29 months in solitary confinement and a mock execution, Bishop Kowalski was expelled in September, 1953. A communist court had branded him an enemy of the

Chinese people; his work with the Legion of Mary was depicted as spying.

When the bishop returned to the United States, he made his home at St. Anthony Friary, his province's novitiate, in Cincinnati. From there he traveled to give retreats, days of recollection, and to administer Confirmations in the Archdiocese of Cincinnati. Bishop Kowalski continued to keep in touch with exiled Chinese missionaries in the United States and abroad. He proudly participated in all four sessions of the Second Vatican Council.

An enthusiastic violinist, the bishop was a joyful man. He had a ready eye for the humor and irony of the human condition. His personal asceticism is best summarized on the cards he passed out at Confirmation:

Talk less...listen more
Look at TV less...think more
Ride less...walk more
Sit less...kneel more
Rest less...work more
Self less...others more
Hate less...love more
Eat less...live longer

Those who lived with him know that he practiced what he preached.

In his later years, the bishop divided his time between the novitiate and St. Michael's Mission in St. Michaels, Arizona. He died there on November 27, 1970.

Quote: After the bishop's death, an autobiography completed in 1968 was found among his effects. Toward the end of that account, he wrote: "Now at the sunset of my 84 years I am convinced that the best and the only thing that one can do is not to oppose the will of God. Because it is certain that God wills only what is best for everyone; because God really wants each and everyone to be with him in heaven forever. Even St. Paul says this as pertaining to everyone: 'I live, now not I but Christ lives in me' [Galatians 2:20]. So if only we let God have the freedom to act in our life, it will be a success. God simply wants our sanctification and our eternal happiness."

Comment: The above quote and the bishop's motto (*Crux mihi dux* — "The cross leads me") summarize his life. His twenty-eight years as bishop of Wuchang were spent almost entirely in prison or in exile. To the end, Bishop Kowalski maintained a great love for the Chinese people, and he prayed daily for their conversion. The cross of Jesus took a somewhat unexpected shape for this missionary follower of Francis, but Bishop Kowalski bore it with tremendous faith.

Blessed Rafal Chyliński (I)
1694-1741

Born near Buk in the Poznań region of Poland, Melchior showed early signs of religious devotion; family members nicknamed him "the little monk." After completing his studies at the Jesuit college in Poznań, Melchior joined the cavalry and was promoted to the rank of officer within three years.

Against the urgings of his military comrades, in 1715 Melchior joined the Conventuals in Kraków, receiving the name Rafal and was ordained two years later. After pastoral assignments in nine cities, he came to Lagiewniki (central Poland), where he spent the last thirteen years of his life, except for twenty months ministering to flood and epidemic victims in Warsaw.

In all these places, Rafal was known for his simple and candid sermons, for his generosity as well as his ministry in the confessional. People of all levels of society were drawn to the self-sacrificing way he lived out his religious profession and priestly ministry.

Rafal played the harp, lute and mandolin to accompany liturgical hymns. In Lagiewniki he distributed food, supplies and clothing to the poor. After his death, the Conventual church in that city became a place of pilgrimage for people throughout Poland. He was beatified in Warsaw in 1991.

Quote: During the beatification homily, Pope John Paul II said, "May Blessed Rafal remind us that every one of us, even though we are sinners, has been called to love and to holiness" (1991 LOR 25:19).

Comment: The sermons preached by Rafal were powerfully reinforced by the living sermon of his life. The Sacrament of Reconciliation can help us bring our daily choices into harmony with our words about Jesus' influence in our life.

Blessed Mary Frances Schervier (III)
1819-1876

This woman who once wanted to become a Trappistine nun was instead led by God to establish a community of sisters who care for the sick and aged in the United States and throughout the world.

Born into a distinguished family in Aix-la-Chapelle, France, Frances ran the household after her mother's death and established a reputation for generosity to the poor. In 1844 she became a Secular Franciscan. The next year she and four companions established a religious community devoted to caring for the poor. In 1851 the Sisters of the Poor of St. Francis were approved by the local bishop; the community soon spread. The first U.S. foundation was made in 1858.

Mother Frances visited the United States in 1863 and helped her sisters nurse soldiers wounded in the Civil War. She visited the United States again in 1868. When Philip Hoever was establishing the Brothers of the Poor of St. Francis, she encouraged him.

When Mother Frances died, there were 2,500 members of her community worldwide. The number has kept growing. They are still engaged in operating hospitals and homes for the aged. Mother Mary Frances was beatified in 1974.

Quote: In 1868, Mother Frances wrote to all her sisters, reminding them of Jesus' words: "You are my friends if you do what I command you.... I am giving you these commands so that you may love one another" (John 15:14,17).

She continued: "If we do this faithfully and zealously, we will experience the truth of the words of our father Saint Francis who says that love lightens all difficulties and sweetens all bitterness. We will likewise partake of the blessing which Saint Francis promised to all his children, both present and future, after having admonished them to love one another even as he had loved them and continues to love them."

Comment: The sick, the poor and the aged are constantly in danger of being considered "useless" members of society and therefore ignored — or worse. Women and men motivated by the ideals of Mother Frances are needed if the God-given dignity and destiny of all people is to be respected.

Blessed Honoratus Kozminski (I)
1829-1916

He was born in Biala Podlaska (Siedlce, Poland) and studied architecture at the School of Fine Arts in Warsaw. When Wenceslaus was almost sixteen, his father died. Suspected of participating in a rebellious conspiracy, the young man was imprisoned from April 1846 until the following March. In 1848 he received the Capuchin habit and a new name. Four years later he was ordained. In 1855 he helped Blessed Mary Angela Truszkowska (October 11) establish the Felician Sisters.

Honoratus served as guardian in a Warsaw friary already in 1860. He dedicated his energies to preaching, to giving spiritual direction and to hearing confessions. He worked tirelessly with the Secular Franciscan Order.

The failed 1864 revolt against Czar Alexander III led to the suppression of all religious Orders in Poland. The Capuchins were expelled from Warsaw and forced to live in Zakroczym, where Honoratus continued his ministry and began founding twenty-six male and female religious congregations, whose members took vows but wore no religious habit and did not live in community. They operated much as today's secular institutes do. Seventeen of these groups still exist as religious congregations.

The writings of Father Honoratus are extensive: forty-two volumes of sermons, twenty-one volumes of letters as well as fifty-two printed works on ascetical theology, Marian devotion, historical writings, pastoral writings — not counting his many writings for the religious congregations he founded.

In 1906, various bishops sought the reorganization of these groups under their authority; Honoratus defended their independence but was removed from their direction in 1908. He promptly urged the members of these congregations to obey the Church's decisions regarding their future.

He "always walked with God," said a contemporary. In 1895 he was appointed Commissary General of the Capuchins in Poland. Three years before he had come to Nowe Miasto, where he died and was buried. He was beatified in 1988.

Quote: When the Church removed Honoratus from the direction of his religious congregations and changed their character, he wrote: "Christ's Vicar himself has revealed God's will to us, and I carry out this order with greatest faith.... Remember, dear brothers and sisters, that you are being given the opportunity to show heroic obedience to the holy Church."

Comment: The story is told that Francis and Brother Leo, his secretary, were once on a journey and Francis volunteered to tell Leo what perfect joy is. Francis began by saying what it was not: news that the kings of France, England, as well as all the world's bishops and many university professors had decided to become friars, news that the friars had received the gift of tongues and miracles, or news that the friars had converted all the non-Christians in the world. No, perfect joy for them would be to arrive cold and hungry at St. Mary of the Angels, Francis' headquarters outside Assisi, and be mistaken by the porter for thieves and beaten by the same porter and driven back into the cold and rain. Francis said that if, for the love of God, he and Leo could endure such treatment without losing their patience and charity, that would be perfect joy (cited in Regis Armstrong, O.F.M. Cap., and Ignatius Brady, O.F.M., *Francis and Clare: The Complete Works*, pages 165-166).

Honoratus worked very zealously to serve the Church, partly by establishing a great variety of religious congregations adapted to the special circumstances of Poland in those years. He could have retreated into bitterness and self-pity when the direction of those congregations was taken away from him; that was certainly a "perfect joy" experience. He urged the members of these groups to obey willingly and gladly, placing their gifts at the service of the Good News of Jesus Christ.

December 18

Mother Alfred Moes (III)
1828-1899

In the year Mother Alfred was born, Andrew Jackson was elected president of the United States and Wisconsin was twenty years away from statehood. The providence of God was to join Europe to the United States through Mother Alfred.

Maria Catherine, the youngest of five girls and three boys, was born in Remich, Luxemburg, to Gerard and Anna Moes. Maria and her sister Catherine entered the convent in Petre (Luxemburg) but did not remain long. Some years later when they met Bishop Martin Henni of Milwaukee, Wisconsin, they decided to go to America and work with Native Americans. In 1852 they entered the School Sisters of Notre Dame in Milwaukee. When again it seemed they lacked a vocation to religious life, the two sisters left that community.

In 1856, Father Edward Sorin, founder of Notre Dame University, invested them as members of the Marianite (later Holy Cross) community. Maria took the name Alfred and Catherine became Barbara. When tensions grew between the Marianite sisters in the United States and their superiors in France, the American sisters were told that they were really not religious and could easily be dispensed from their vows.

Under the direction of Father Pamfilo da Magliano (November 16), Sister Alfred and Sister Barbara established in Joliet, Illinois, the Sisters of the Third Order of Saint Francis of Mary Immaculate. In 1865, Sister Alfred was appointed mother superior of this community of Franciscan sisters dedicated to teaching.

Divisions within the community, however, cost her dearly. When some sisters complained that Mother Alfred had never been elected as mother superior, the bishop of Joliet ordered an election. Mother Alfred's name was withheld from the ballot.

She was then sent to Owatana, Minnesota, to build and run a girls' academy. Misunderstandings with the Joliet community led to a separation; in Rochester, Minnesota, several sisters formed a new community under the patronage of Our Lady of Lourdes. This community serves in schools, hospitals, homes for the aged and in pastoral ministries. Mother Alfred was instrumental in the founding of the world famous Mayo Clinic in Rochester, Minnesota.

Quote: Mother Alfred's motto was "To think is to do."

Comment: Mother Alfred continually sought the best way she could serve God. Though this search led her through several religious communities, she enriched each one of them by her prayer and self-sacrifice. These made her sensitive to the needs of God's people. Her work was done with all the generosity of Francis and Clare.

Franciscan Calendar

January
3   Holy Name of Jesus (Memorial)
7   Blessed Angela of Foligno
12 Blessed Bernard of Corleone
14 Blessed Odoric of Pordenone
16 Berard and Companions (Memorial)
30 Hyacintha of Mariscotti

February
4   Joseph of Leonissa
6   Peter Baptist, Paul Miki and Companions (Memorial)
7   Colette
19 Conrad of Piacenza

March
2   Agnes of Bohemia
24 Blessed Didacus Joseph of Cadiz

April
3   Benedict the African (Memorial)
21 Conrad of Parzham (Memorial)
23 Blessed Giles of Assisi
24 Fidelis of Sigmaringen (Feast)
28 Blessed Luchesio

May
9   Catharine of Bologna
11 Ignatius of Laconi
16 Margaret of Cortona (Memorial)
17 Paschal Baylon (Memorial)
18 Felix of Cantalice (Feast)
20 Bernardine of Siena (Feast)
24 Dedication of the Basilica of Saint Francis of Assisi (Feast)
28 Mary Ann of Jesus of Paredes
30 Blessed Baptista Varano

June
12 Blessed Jolenta
13 Anthony of Padua (Feast)
30 Blessed Raymond Lull

July

1 Blessed Junipero Serra
8 Blessed Gregory Grassi and Companions
9 Nicholas Pick and Companions (Memorial)
10 Veronica Giuliani (Memorial)
12 John Jones and John Wall
13 Blessed Angeline of Marsciano
14 Francis Solano
15 Bonaventure (Feast)
21 Lawrence of Brindisi (Feast)
23 Blessed Cunegunda
24 Blessed Louise of Savoy
27 Blessed Mary Magdalene of Martinengo

August

2 Our Lady of the Angels of Portiuncula (Feast)
7 Blesseds Agathangelus and Cassian
8 Dominic (Feast)
11 Clare of Assisi (Feast)
14 Maximilian Mary Kolbe
19 Louis of Toulouse (Memorial)
25 Louis IX (Memorial)

September

1 Blessed Beatrice of Silva
2 Blessed John Francis Burté and Companions
4 Rose of Viterbo
17 Stigmata of Saint Francis (Feast)
18 Joseph of Cupertino (Feast)
20 Francis Mary of Camporosso (Memorial)
23 Finding of the Body of Saint Clare
26 Elzear of Sabran and Blessed Delphina

October

4 Francis of Assisi (Solemnity)
6 Mary Frances of the Five Wounds
10 Daniel and Companions
12 Seraphin of Montegranaro
13 Blessed James of Strepar
Blessed Contardo Ferrini
21 Blessed Josephine Leroux
22 Peter of Alcantara (Memorial)

23   John of Capistrano (Memorial)
26   Blessed Bonaventure of Potenza
30   Anniversary of the Dedication of the Consecrated Churches
        of the Order (Solemnity)

November
7   Didacus of Alcalá
14   Nicholas Tavelić and Companions (Memorial)
17   Elizabeth of Hungary (Feast)
18   Blessed Salome
19   Agnes of Assisi
24   Commemoration of the Deceased of the Seraphic Order
        (Memorial)
26   Leonard of Port Maurice (Memorial)
27   Francesco Antonio Fasani
28   James of the Marche (Memorial)
29   All the Saints of the Seraphic Order (Feast)

December
15   Blessed Mary Frances Schervier

Bibliography

Five sources were especially helpful in the writing of this book:

Armstrong, Regis, O.F.M. Cap., and Ignatius Brady, O.F.M. *Francis and Clare: The Complete Works* (New York: Paulist Press, 1982).

Flannery, Austin, O.P., ed. *Vatican Council II: The Conciliar and Post Conciliar Documents* (Northport, N.Y.: Costello Publishing Co., 1996). Citations from Vatican II documents are from this source, revised for inclusive language.

Habig, Marion A., O.F.M. *The Franciscan Book of Saints* (Chicago: Franciscan Herald Press, revised edition, 1979). This book presents a Franciscan Saint, Blessed, Venerable or Servant of God for each day of the year and offers an extensive bibliography on Franciscan Saints and Blesseds.

Habig, Marion A., O.F.M., ed. *St. Francis of Assisi: Writings and Early Biographies, English Omnibus of the Sources for the Life of St Francis* (Chicago: Franciscan Herald Press, revised edition, 1977).

New Catholic Encyclopedia (New York: McGraw-Hill, 1967).

Other Sources
Books

Beraud de Saint-Maurice. *John Duns Scotus: A Teacher For Our Times*, translated by Columban Duffy, O.F.M. (St. Bonaventure, N.Y.: Franciscan Institute, 1955).

Biersack, Louis, O.F.M. Cap. *The Saints and Blesseds of the Third Order of St. Francis* (Paterson, N.J.: St. Anthony Guild Press, 1943).

Bodo, Murray, O.F.M. *Clare: A Light in the Garden* (Cincinnati: St. Anthony Messenger Press, revised edition, 1992).

_____. *Francis: The Journey and the Dream* (Cincinnati: St. Anthony Messenger Press, revised edition, 1988).

Brady, Ignatius, O.F.M. *The Legend and Writings of St. Clare of Assisi* (St. Bonaventure, N.Y.: Franciscan Institute, 1953).

Brown, Raphael. *The Wounded Heart* [biography of Charles of Sezze] (Chicago: Franciscan Herald Press, 1960).

_____. *Franciscan Mystic* [biography of Brother Giles] (New York: Hanover House, 1962).

Carney, Margaret, O.S.F. *The First Franciscan Woman: Clare of Assisi and Her Form of Life* (Quincy, Ill.: Franciscan Press, 1993).

Carty, Charles Mortimer. *Padre Pio the Stigmatist* (Minneapolis: Radio Replies Press, 5th ed., 1953).

Chesterton, Gilbert Keith. *Orthodoxy* (Garden City, N.Y.: Doubleday and Company, 1959).

Cousins, Ewart, trans. Bonaventure: *The Soul's Journey Into God, The Tree of Life, The Life of St. Francis* (New York: Paulist Press, 1978).

De Lubac, Henri, S.J. *The Splendor of the Church*, trans. Michael Mason (Glen Rock, N.J.: Paulist Press, 1963).

Derum, James Patrick. *The Porter of St. Bonaventure's* [biography of Solanus Casey] (Detroit: Fidelity Press, 1968).

Englebert, Omer. *Saint Francis of Assisi: A Biography*, trans. Eve Marie Cooper, second English edition, revised and augmented by Ignatius Brady, O.F.M., and Raphael Brown (Chicago: Franciscan Herald Press, 1965).

Foley, Leonard, O.F.M., ed. *Saint of the Day* (Cincinnati: St. Anthony Messenger Press, revised edition, 1990).

Geiger, Maynard, O.F.M., trans. & ed. *Palou's Life of Fray Junipero Serra* (Washington, D.C.: Academy of American Franciscan History, 1954).

_____. *The Life and Times of Junipero Serra, or The Man Who Never Turned Back*, two volumes (Washington, D.C.: Academy of American Franciscan History, 1959).

Habig, Marion A., O.F.M. *In Journeyings Often: Franciscan Pioneers in the Orient* (St. Bonaventure, N.Y.: Franciscan Institute, 1953).

_____. *Saints of the Americas* (Huntington, Ind.: Our Sunday Visitor, 1974).

Hanley, Boniface, O.F.M. *Ten Christians* (South Bend, Ind.: Ave Maria Press, 1979).

John Paul II. *Gift and Mystery: On the Fiftieth Anniversay of My Priestly Ordination* (New York: Doubleday, 1996).

_____. *Redemptor Hominis* [Redeemer of Man] (Boston: Daughters of St. Paul, 1979).

Leon (de Clary), Pere, O.F.M. *Lives of the Saints and Blesseds of the Three Orders of Saint Francis*, 4 volumes, translated from *Aureole Seraphique* (Taunton, England: Franciscan Convent, 1885-87).

McCloskey, Pat, O.F.M. *St. Anthony of Padua: Wisdom For Today* (Cincinnati: St. Anthony Messenger Press, 1977).

Nevins, Albert, M.M. *American Martyrs From 1542* (Huntington, Ind.: Our Sunday Visitor, 1987).

Perotti, Leonard. *St. Charles of Sezze: An Autobiography* (London: Burns & Oates, 1963).

Rahner, Karl. *Theological Dictionary*, trans. Richard Strachen (New York: Herder and Herder, 1965).

Ricard, Robert. *The Spiritual Conquest of Mexico: An Essay on the Apostolate and the Evangelizing Methods of the Mendicant Orders in New Spain — 1523-1572*, translated by Lesley Byrd Simpson (Berkeley, Calif.: University of California Press, 1966).

Robinson, Paschal, O.F.M., trans. and ed. *Golden Sayings of Brother Giles* (Philadelphia: Philadelphia Press, 1907).

Tutu, Right Rev. Desmond Mpilo. *Hope and Suffering* (Grand Rapids, Mich.: William B. Eerdmans Co., 1984).

Voillaume, Rene. *Brothers of Men: Letters to the Petits Frères* (Baltimore: Helicon Press, 1966).

Winowska, Maria. *Go...Repair My House: Biography of Mother Mary Angela Truszkowska* (Lodi, N.J.: Congregation of the Sisters of St. Felix, 1976).

Pamphlets and Articles

Brady, Ignatius, O.F.M. "St. Francis and the Holy Spirit," *Sursum Corda* 14:5, pp. 214-21.

Foley, Leonard, O.F.M. "St. Leonard of Port Maurice" (Cincinnati: St. John the Baptist Province, 1959).

Hanley, Boniface, O.F.M. *Anthonian* (Paterson, N.J.): 47.4 (Maximilian Kolbe); 50:4 (Frederick Ozanam); 52:3 (Margaret Sinclair); 46:2 (Matt Talbot); and 50:1 (John Vianney).

Hanley, Sister Laurence, O.S.F. "Mother Marianne of Molokai" (Syracuse, N.Y.: 1977).

Kowalski, Rembert, O.F.M. "A Franciscan Bishop Tells His Story" (Cincinnati: St. Anthony Friary, 1972).

Wroblewski, Sergius, O.F.M. "Sons of Saint Francis: Get Together" (Pulaski: Franciscan Publishers, 1980).

Zarrella, Mary Alice. "I Will...God's Will: A Biography of Mother Mary Maddalena Bentivoglio, O.S.C." (Evansville, Ind.: Poor Clare Monastery Press, 1975).

Index